GUIDING YOUR
CHURCH THROUGH A
WORSHIP
TRANSITION

A PRACTICAL HANDBOOK
FOR WORSHIP RENEWAL

TOM KRAEUTER

Emerald Books

P.O. BOX 635, LYNNWOOD, WA 98046

Training Resources
Hillsboro, Missouri

Emerald Books are distributed through YWAM Publishing. For a full list of titles, including other great worship resources, visit our website at www.ywampublishing.com or call 1-800-922-2143.

Guiding Your Church through a Worship Transition: A Practical Handbook for Worship Renewal

Copyright © 2003 by Training Resources, Inc.

> 8929 Old LeMay Ferry Road
> Hillsboro, MO 63050
> (636) 789-4522
> www.training-resources.org

10 09 08 07 06 05 04 03   10 9 8 7 6 5 4 3 2 1

Published by Emerald Books
P.O. Box 635
Lynnwood, Washington 98046

ISBN 1-932096-08-6

Library of Congress Cataloging-in-Publication Data
has been applied for.

Printed in the United States of America.

I humbly dedicate this book to my oldest son, David Kraeuter.

Through the years I have found that raising children is much like the process of guiding a church. Love, prayer, a strong adherence to the principles of God's Word, laughing (and sometimes crying), working together, and even an occasional bit of friction are all part of the process.

David, I'm so glad that God entrusted you into our care for a time. I have learned much about life from our interaction. I'm very proud to call you my son.

OTHER BOOKS BY TOM KRAEUTER

ACKNOWLEDGMENTS

Thanks to:

Those who offered so many worthwhile ideas for this book including (but not limited to):

John Barcanic
Jim Barnes
John Chevalier
Joel Christiansen
Phil Mahder
Joel Ragains
Richard Webb

Those who reviewed the manuscript ahead of time and offered suggestions:

Gerry Clemmer, Mennonite
Paula Haddix, Lutheran
Ann McNerney, Church of the Brethren
Justin Miller, Christian Church
Randy Mitrovich, Baptist
Cary Mock, United Methodist

The scores of pastors and worship leaders who allowed me to ask them *lots* of questions about their experiences.

Rory Noland for graciously writing the foreword.

Jennifer Brody, my favorite editor!

Emerald Books for having enough confidence in my writing to publish yet another book by me.

Special thanks to my wife, Barbara, and our children, David, Stephen, and Amy, for loving me and allowing me the time to complete this manuscript.

CONTENTS

FOREWORD

We've all seen it happen before, and some of us have seen it happen often. A pastor attends a church growth conference and returns with dozens of new ideas that he's eager to implement. Or a recently hired worship leader announces that he or she is taking the ministry in "a new direction." In both cases, change is afoot and controversy ensues. Some in the congregation are excited. They rally around the new approach to ministry with full support. Others wonder what's wrong with the way the church has been doing ministry all along. They view the new direction as a trendy compromise of foundational spiritual values. Still others are suspicious of the leader's motives. They accuse the pastor or the worship leader of trying to make a name for themselves. Then there is a group of people in the middle who take a "wait and see" approach. They're not going to commit either way until they see how the controversy plays out.

Very few people handle change well. It's a paradox within human nature. We love variety, but we hate change. We love new things, but we're uncomfortable with something if it's unfamiliar. We hate the status quo, but we love the security it offers. By the same token, the Church has never been famous for handling change well, and church music has been in the thick of many a battle.

That's where Tom Kraeuter's book *Guiding Your Church through a Worship Transition* comes in. I haven't run across any other book about this crucial topic that is as thorough as this one is. Drawing from his broad experience, as well as the wisdom of Scripture, Tom gets to the heart of the matter and offers very practical advice. If every church navigated change the way Tom outlines, it would save all of us a great deal of pain and heartache.

My first encounter with Tom occurred when I attended one of his worship workshops in Chicago. Since then we've become good friends, and we've also had the opportunity to minister together. Tom is a godly man and a gifted teacher who's deeply committed to the local church. He offers a wealth of knowledge, a storehouse of ministry experience, and perceptive insights. His sense of humor is endearing, and his enthusiasm for worship is contagious. All the things that make his teaching so deeply effective come across in his writing.

It is the responsibility of every leader to initiate and manage change in a way that preserves the beauty of the Bride of Christ. That's why every leader should have this book within reach at all times.

RORY NOLAND

Music Director, Willow Creek Community Church
Author, *The Heart of the Artist*

INTRODUCTION

Throughout the Church today, God is renewing worship. There is an increasing emphasis on worship being heartfelt as well as relevant to the twenty-first-century Christian. Mainline churches, evangelicals, and Pentecostals alike are all examining not only the style of their worship but also how the entire worship experience relates to those living in modern-day society. If these ideas interest you, then this book will offer practical help.

My goal in writing this book is not to push any specific agenda. I am not necessarily trying to get you to embrace wholeheartedly a particular style of music in your church's congregational worship. The specific style is far less important than whether or not it is relevant to the people to whom you are ministering.

The truth is that this has been a very awkward book for me to write. Echoing a statement I heard years ago, I have often said that if someone were to cut open my teaching, I'd like it to bleed Scripture. If you've read any of my other writings, you know that I have endeavored to achieve this goal.

This book, however, is very different. In fact, many—perhaps most—of the things in this book are not even mentioned, let alone defined, in the Bible. Because of this, I have had to draw on my own experiences in churches across North America, as well as the experiences of others. I interviewed pastors and worship leaders from various backgrounds, attempting to verify my suppositions as well as to find out what I was missing.

Therefore much of the information in this book is based on experience, not Scripture. I have neither forgotten nor neglected the Word of God. Where there is a scriptural basis for something, I have included it. However, I have seen too many teachers who have twisted verses from the Bible to make them fit a particular agenda. I refuse to do this.

I hope and pray that the information contained herein will prove beneficial to many congregations.

CHAPTER 1

DON'T PUT NEW PAINT
ON ROTTING WOOD

🌿 *The Cornerstone of*
Relationship with God

When I was a young boy, nearly every summer our family visited my grandparents' farm in northwestern Pennsylvania. They had a huge red barn with a hayloft and *lots* of hiding places. Farm animals were everywhere, and there were more acres to explore than a kid like me could possibly have visited in the week we were there.

One of the things I remember best about the farm was the cabin. It was a ramshackle structure in the woods beyond the pasture. The cabin was actually two stories tall, though I don't recall ever being in the upper level, probably because it wasn't safe. Some of the kids (I was the youngest of five) always had ideas about how to fix up the cabin. Maybe a couple of nails here, a little paint over there. How about some plastic over the roof?

These cosmetic measures would make the cabin look a bit nicer—temporarily. The real problem, however, was not being addressed. You can't fix a structure that is rotting by covering it with some paint. Nails driven into termite-infested wood won't add much stability. You can make things look a little prettier for a while, but unless the real problem is addressed, it won't make any significant difference.

Over the years, people have frequently asked me about changing the style of music in their services. They want to move from the traditional music that seemingly has been a part of their church forever into a more culturally relevant style of music. Unfortunately, they are often trying to address a deeper issue with a surface treatment.

"There seems to be somewhat of a lethargic attitude in our congregation. People come to the service(s), but they just don't seem to be connected to what's going on. We think that if we make the music a bit more contemporary, it will help people. What do you think about that idea?"

If worship were predominantly a music issue, it might work. If all God were interested in was people singing and clapping in time to the music, then using a more familiar style of music just might be the key. From the Lord's perspective, however, that is clearly not the main issue. Worship, at its essence, is a heart issue. You cannot begin dealing with an internal issue from an external perspective. That's like putting some fresh paint on rotting wood. It may look nice for a time, but the real problem has not been addressed.

Make no mistake: before we can talk about music, we must first talk about heart. Stephen Charnock, a Puritan who lived during the seventeenth century, said this: "Without the heart, it is not worship; it is a stage play, an acting part... We may be truly said to worship God, though we [lack] perfection; but we cannot be said to worship Him if we [lack] sincerity."[1]

Centuries ago God addressed this topic in very clear terms. He spoke these words through the prophet Isaiah:

> Hear the word of the LORD, you rulers of Sodom;
> listen to the law of our God, you people of
> Gomorrah!

Before we go too far here, let me interject that God is not speaking to Sodom and Gomorrah in these verses. He is addressing His chosen people, Israel, but He is not very happy with them. He has resorted to calling them names!

> "The multitude of your sacrifices—what are they to me?" says the LORD. "I have more than enough of burnt offerings, of rams and the fat of fattened animals; I have no pleasure in the blood of bulls and lambs and goats. When you come to appear before me, who has asked this of you, this trampling of my courts? Stop bringing meaningless offerings! Your incense is detestable to me. New Moons, Sabbaths and convocations—I cannot bear your evil assemblies. Your New Moon festivals and

your appointed feasts my soul hates. They have become a burden to me; I am weary of bearing them" (Isaiah 1:10–14).

When I read this section of Scripture, my initial reaction is, "Wait a minute! Who was it who had asked for all these things? Who had requested the incense and offerings, the festivals and feasts, the sacrifices—who asked for all of these?" It was God. Yet here He is saying, "Stop! I don't want them!" But why? Were the people performing these rituals incorrectly?

No. In fact, looking at the history of Israel, I honestly can't believe it was because they were doing any of these things wrong. By the time the Lord spoke these words, the Israelites were probably so good at these rituals that they could do them without even thinking about them. That was the problem. They were going through the motions but without the heart. They were doing all of the things that God had told them to do, but their hearts were not turned toward Him. In essence God said, "I'm not interested in the externals; I want your heart." Later in the book of Isaiah, the Lord says this very thing: "These people come near to me with their mouth and honor me with their lips, but their hearts are far from me" (Isaiah 29:13).

If people don't have a living, vibrant relationship with the Lord, changing the style of music will have little long-term effect. In their classic book, *Worship: Rediscovering the Missing Jewel*, Ronald Allen and Gordon Borror state it this way: "The real factor in worship is a heart desire for

God; the reason it fails to occur in the pew is because it fails to occur in the daily routine of living."[2]

I recently read a magazine article in which Tricia McCary Rhodes shared a great analogy regarding this issue.

> Years ago, as missionaries in the Alaskan wilderness, my husband and I drew our water from an indoor pump. We were city folk, and at first we didn't understand the pump's mechanics. Once a week, we poured in a cup of water to prime it, pumped like crazy until water sprung up from underground, then filled every bucket and pot we could find.
>
> I well remember how an Eskimo neighbor laughed at our system. Then he explained that if we used the pump whenever we needed, it would always stay primed, ready to gush out with one easy thrust of the handle.[3]

True worship must be understood in these terms also. Priming the pump once a week and pumping like crazy is clearly no substitute for an ongoing relationship with the Lord. Changing music styles will not make a difference in people unless their hearts are turned toward God. Conversely, when the hearts of the people are focused on the Lord, the style of music becomes secondary. Allen and Borror put it rather succinctly when they wrote, "When the heart is set upon God, true worship will not depend upon outward stimulus, it will be in constant progress."[4]

Guiding Your Church through a Worship Transition

Actually, without a deepening relationship with Christ, changes can seem even more threatening to people. One worship leader said it like this: "When people do not grasp the heart relationship—when it is totally a head knowledge understanding of God with no real relationship—for them, changing the style of worship is a threat." It's true. When the heart relationship is right, the changes are much easier to make.

We must never think that changing the style of music or using modern language in our services will somehow automatically cause spirituality to increase. Before we can talk about issues of style, we must first put into place the foundational issue—a relationship with God through the death and resurrection of Jesus Christ.

Since this book is being written predominantly to leaders in churches, let me first address you as a leader. What is your relationship with God like? Is the Lord the focus of *your* everyday life? The old axiom is true: you can't take someone to a place if you don't know the way. If you, the leader, do not have a vibrant relationship with God, your people most likely will not either.

In his book *Seven Seasons of the Man in the Mirror*, Patrick Morley made a powerful observation.

Statistically, it appears America has undergone a religious revival. On further reflection, however, we learn there is more to it. As the children of the baby boomers grow up, their moms and dads want them to have religious and moral instruction. So the baby boomers are rejoining the church they abandoned when they went off to college.

In days gone by, a person had to confess faith in Christ before joining the church. Not so today. Because of the low to no prerequisites for joining the body of Christ, many churches are top heavy with people who don't know God personally. On top of that, because of a low view of God in many churches, there is a plethora of Cultural Christians —some of whom we might call mature infants in Christ, and some don't even know Him at all. They know *about* God, but they don't know *Him*.[5]

Clearly, the place to begin in this entire issue is stressing the heart relationship with God. Don't simply try to put fresh paint onto rotting wood. An authentic, biblical relationship with Christ is the cornerstone that must be in place before the rest of the structure can be built.

CHAPTER 2

WHY DON'T YOUR PANTS HAVE HOLES IN THE KNEES?

🔥 *Prayer, the Foundation*

I have a habit of getting an idea—especially something I perceive to be a good, even godly, idea—and running with it. God has gifted me with enough charisma, intelligence, and poise to be able to get other people excited about the idea quickly. I can string words together in such a way that people can become convinced that this idea is something in which they really should be involved. Making ideas become reality is not a terribly difficult thing for me.

However, over the years I have too frequently run roughshod over someone else's feelings in an attempt to make my ideas happen. Those who are not immediately willing participants have been branded as opposition. Anyone not in agreement has been ignored or even vilified.

Now don't sit there smugly thinking what a good person you are compared with me. If you have been in a leadership position for any length of time, you've probably done something similar at some point. You may not have been as blatant. Underneath, however, there is often a conniving and scheming attitude that, from God's perspective, is exactly the same.

What I—and perhaps you—have too often missed is prayer. Without this underlying foundation, we will never fully accomplish the plans and purposes of God. Oh, we may sway people for a time—perhaps even a long time— but only God can create deep, wholesale, permanent changes in individuals, in congregations, and in us.

Years ago, in the midst of my usual busy schedule, one day I had not taken the time to pray. I looked back over the years of my life and ministry and realized that this was not an uncommon occurrence. Then I made a statement I will probably always regret: "But, Lord, look how much You have accomplished through me even without my taking the necessary time to pray." Immediately I realized what a foolish statement it was. I knew the converse was also true: what far more amazing things could God have accomplished in and through me if I had taken the time to pray?

Jesus told us, "Apart from me you can do nothing" (John 15:5b). There is nothing of any lasting value that you and I will ever accomplish without the Lord somehow being involved. And that involvement should not be an accidental, "O God, I'm so glad You're a part of this; I almost forgot about You." We absolutely must be deliberate in our asking for His guidance, wisdom, understanding, heart, strength, attitude, etc. The bottom line is, we need to pray.

Let's be honest, though. Too often we don't pray because we don't always see immediate results from our prayers. Donald Whitney said it this way:

> Often we do not pray because we doubt that anything will actually happen if we pray. Of course, we don't admit this publicly. But if we felt certain of visible results within sixty seconds of every prayer, there would be holes in the knees of every pair of Christian-owned pants in the world![1]

In his excellent book *The Joy of Fearing God*, author and teacher Jerry Bridges expressed it perhaps even more candidly:

> Unfortunately our degree of trust in God often lies more in our ability to foresee a way in which He might answer our prayers than in our belief in His power. If we can't see *how* He can answer, we tend to doubt that He *will* answer. We pray, but if we were really honest with God and expressed our thoughts, this is how it would come out: "You know, Lord, that it's a long shot. I don't see how You can possibly accomplish it, but I'm going to pray for it and see if something just might happen."[2]

At this point I could launch into a lengthy dissertation about how God expects us to pray in faith (Matthew 21:22; Mark 11:24), and how He clearly does not like the kind of prayer mentioned above (James 1:6–8). However, one of the things that I so appreciate about God is that He takes us right where we are and leads us on from there. More times than I could tell, when I lacked faith, God still answered. He is faithful. Even when we are faithless, the Lord is still faithful (2 Timothy 2:13). So pray.

God's Word repeatedly tells us to pray. "Therefore I tell you, whatever you ask for in prayer, believe that you have received it, and it will be yours" (Mark 11:24). "And if we know that he hears us—whatever we ask—we know that we have what we asked of him" (1 John 5:15). "You have granted him the desire of his heart and have not withheld the request of his lips" (Psalm 21:2).

Paul, the apostle, frequently requested prayer (see Ephesians 6:19–20; Colossians 4:3–4; 1 Thessalonians 5:25). Jesus modeled the necessity of prayer: "But Jesus often withdrew to lonely places and prayed" (Luke 5:16).

When I read books and magazines, I frequently make notes of quotes that I think are worthwhile for future use. Usually I also record information about the author and publication in which the quote appeared. Once in a while I inadvertently omit this step. This quote is one for which I neglected to obtain the source information. However, it is so pertinent to my point that I thought I should share it anyway.

Mining is hard work. Boring into solid rock is no easy task. It requires patience and commitment, but it is essential to the mining process. Once the boring is complete, a charge is placed in the hole, and large amounts of rock are then blasted away. If the blast occurred on the surface, it would not have the same impact. Many Christians today are eager to participate in lighting the fuse, but few are willing to give themselves to the difficult job of boring into solid rock. Anyone can light the fuse. It takes commitment and patience to do the hard work.

The hard work is prayer. The commitment to prayer will make a gigantic difference in how your congregation responds to your attempts to move forward.

So, where should our focus be in prayer? In other words, what should we pray for?

To start with, we should pray for ourselves. We really need to ask God to keep us going in the right direction. We can have some wonderfully creative ideas, but the more important question is, are they God-inspired ideas? This can be a difficult lesson to learn. Our ideas always seem like good ideas—to us. However, we need to be honestly open to the Lord adjusting, altering, or even voiding our plans. There is no way we can ask God to bless what we are doing unless we are willing to accept His guidance and correction. We need to surrender willingly to the Lord, asking to be a vessel that He uses to bring about His plans and purposes.

Once we have sincerely prayed for ourselves to be following the Lord's guidance, we also need to pray for the hearts of our congregation to be open to where God is leading. As I mentioned earlier, we may be able to sway some of the people to our way of thinking, but only God can make truly lasting changes in heart, in attitudes, and in thinking. We must ask Him to prepare people for the direction in which we are headed as a congregation so they will be willing to follow.

Sometimes we are concerned about the reaction of a particular person or group of people because of past interaction with that person or group. "They bucked us the last time we tried to make a change," we reason, "and they will probably do it again." It is prayer that will make the difference.

Carl George is a well-known and highly respected church conflict consultant. He firmly believes prayer is essential in dealing with congregational conflicts. He said, "Flat out, it's the largest single solution to the majority of divisive problems I've seen in the church. But a breakthrough occurs only when somebody decides to pay the price in prayer."[3]

Hmmm. Paying the price in prayer sounds like the boring-into-solid-rock hard work of prayer we talked about earlier. Prayer is not necessarily easy, but it is very effective. The Almighty Lord of the Universe is waiting for us to call on Him in prayer. Let's do it.

Begin with the cornerstone of relationship with the Lord. Then lay the foundation of prayer. It is only after these are in place that you are ready to move forward.

CHAPTER 3

DEFACING THE TEMPLE

🌿 *A Better Way: Love*

Have you ever walked into church on Sunday morning and thought (or said) something negative about a brother or sister in Christ? Perhaps something like "There's Joe. I wish he'd grow up, get his hair cut, and act like a normal Christian." Or "There's Sue. She must be one of the strangest people I've ever met." Have you ever done that or anything like that? If you have, what was the outcome? Whether you realized it or not, you put a wall between yourself and that person.

Harboring negative attitudes toward one another can hinder us in moving forward in our worship. Actually, the truth is, they *will* hinder it. This is a major but often overlooked piece of the puzzle that needs to be in place in order to truly move forward in our worship.

In the second chapter of his letter to the believers in Ephesus, Paul discusses the concept of the Church being built together into a holy temple. He concludes this section by saying, "And in Him you too are being built together to become a dwelling in which God lives by His Spirit" (Ephesians 2:22). For most Christians, this idea is not new. Honestly, the concept that God is building us together is a foundational teaching of the Church. It is found in both the Old and New Testaments. Different terminology is used in different places, but ultimately it is the same idea: God is building us together. To me this is so fundamental that I would consider it a part of "Basic Christianity 101."

However, even when we understand that God is indeed building us together, we often miss His purpose in doing it. Why is He making us into a building? The answer is found in the second chapter of Peter's first letter. "You also, like living stones, are being built into a spiritual house to be a holy priesthood, offering spiritual sacrifices acceptable to God through Jesus Christ" (1 Peter 2:5). "…a holy priesthood offering spiritual sacrifices…"? That sounds like worship. Of course it is. That is what we are all about as God's people. The reason that the Lord is building us together into a building is that we might worship Him.

If this is true (and obviously it is, since Scripture says so), it follows logically that if the building is not built properly, then the spiritual sacrifices will be lacking. If our relationships with one another are out of order, then the purpose of the building will not be fulfilled.

This is quite contrary to our normal way of thinking. More frequently we consider all of the other options. If the worship for a given service seems "flat," our first tendency is to think, "Well, I guess the person leading worship didn't hear from God this week." However, our first course of action should be to look into our own heart. We should consider our relationships with our brothers and sisters.

In his first letter to the Corinthian church, Paul said, "Don't you know that you yourselves are God's temple and that God's Spirit lives in you? If anyone destroys God's temple, God will destroy him; for God's temple is sacred, and you [plural] are that temple" (1 Corinthians 3:16–17).

The Greek word here for destroying the temple literally means to "corrupt" or to "mar." In Bible times, if anyone was caught doing any type of damage to the temple—writing graffiti on the walls, for example—there was an instant death sentence pronounced. If you were caught, there was no question in anyone's mind what the outcome would be. Your life was over.

However, we do that very thing when we come to church harboring negative attitudes toward our brothers and sisters in Christ. We are corrupting, marring, destroying the temple into which the Lord is building us. Even if this is not our intent, we can unknowingly destroy the temple by harboring resentments and other negative attitudes toward others.

I am not trying to say that we must have extremely close relationships with everyone we know. This is impossible. It seems obvious that there are various levels of relationship. We can see this even in the life of Jesus. Multitudes followed Him. Out of those multitudes, He appointed seventy-two followers and sent them out two by two (Luke 10:1–20). From among these, He chose twelve apostles. But even among these there was an "inner circle" of three—Peter, James, and John—who were nearly always with Jesus. Finally, the Bible refers only to John as the disciple "Jesus loved," suggesting a special relationship between Jesus and John. Obviously, we too have various levels of relationships.

While we need to understand this, it also presents a danger to us. We can begin to view some relationships as unimportant. Be honest. Are there certain people in the body of Christ you have difficulty relating to? Are there some folks with whom you even avoid making eye contact in order to keep from talking with them?

After many years as a Christian, I finally came to the realization that on this side of eternity I would never see eye to eye with everyone in the kingdom of God. The truth is that being in complete agreement is of very little consequence. What really matters is that I understand that Jesus paid just as much for those people with whom I do not fully agree as He did for me. This mind-set quickly changes my perspective on people. I make the choice to walk in love and unity with my brothers and sisters in the Lord.

All too often, we Christians act as though Jesus told us that people would know we are His disciples because we all agree on everything doctrinally. He didn't say that.

He told us, "By this all men will know that you are My disciples, if you *love one another*" (John 13:35, author's emphasis).

I am not suggesting that doctrine is unimportant. As a teacher in the body of Christ, I recognize that doctrine is extremely important. If I didn't think so, I would not be doing what I'm doing. It is imperative—especially in this hour—that we as the Church know what we believe and why we believe it, firmly based on the Word of God. However, perfect doctrinal agreement is not the high-water mark of the Church of Jesus Christ. 1 Corinthians 13 says, "If I...can fathom all mysteries and all knowledge...*but have not love*, I am nothing" (1 Corinthians 13:2, author's emphasis).

So, you might be wondering, what does all this have to do with worship? Simple. Jesus told us, "If you are offering your gift at the altar and there remember that your brother has something against you, leave your gift there in front of the altar. First go and be reconciled to your brother; then come and offer your gift" (Matthew 5:23–24). Before we can worship, we need to be careful to ensure that our relationships are in order.

John is even stronger in his treatment of this subject. "Anyone who does not love his brother, whom he has seen, cannot love God, whom he has not seen" (1 John 4:20b). This verse doesn't say that if we don't love our brother, then we *might not* be able to love God. It says that if we don't love our brother, we *cannot* love God. The Lord has tied our relationship with Him to our relationships with one another. Unquestionably, if our horizontal relationships with one another are not in proper order, then we cannot have the vertical relationship with God.

Allow me a few moments to put this into a positive context. In my travels I have encountered congregations where the more mature believers (when I speak here of maturity, I am not necessarily talking about age, but you and I both recognize that maturity generally comes with age) have come to the point of recognizing that they have a choice. The first option is that their church can continue doing things the way they have always done them—their preferences, their opinions—and die with them when they die. The second option is to give up their preferences and opinions to encourage the next generation in their walk with the Lord.

Where they have made that latter choice, giving up their preferences and ways of doing things, there comes a dynamic in the unity of the church and therefore a dynamic in the corporate expression of worship that cannot be achieved any other way. Why? Because it speaks volumes to the less mature believers when we more mature believers are willing to give up our opinions and choices to help them. Reaching out in love causes us to discard our us-against-them mentality. They, in turn, begin to have an attitude that says, "We don't always have to do things our way." There springs forth a give and take, a caring for one another, that won't happen any other way. This love automatically carries over into the corporate expression of worship.

If we are honestly going to move forward in worship as a congregation, then we must foster loving, caring relationships among our people. Without this we're just a resounding gong or a clanging cymbal (1 Corinthians 13:1). We must be careful not to deface the temple we build on the foundations of relationship with Christ and prayer.

CHAPTER 4

ARE YOU SURE YOU WANT TO DO THIS?

❦ Why Even Make a Change?

Unless you have some kind of martyr complex, you probably are not wanting to make a change in worship styles just for the fun of the challenge. Unquestionably, the first thing you'll encounter in bringing up the subject of culturally relevant worship is that people have an opinion. This is not a topic for a polite Sunday afternoon conversation over tea. Most people feel very strongly persuaded in one direction or the other, and they are usually not shy about voicing that opinion.

Moreover the argument about worship styles is clearly not new. It seems to have been a recurring theme throughout the history of the church. It's been repeated over and over again.

Recently I was having supper with some leadership people from a particular denomination. As we ate and talked, one man lamented the fact that in some of their churches there are folks who want to throw out the new hymnal from the late-1990s and return to the older hymnal from the 1950s. Apparently they don't like the fact that the new hymnal contains several modern choruses. Suddenly one of the men who knew a bit of the church's history asked, "Do you know why that 1950s hymnal was originally commissioned?" None of the rest of us had any idea, so he told us. "It was a reaction to the hymnal from the early 1900s that many people thought contained too many choruses." We were all stunned. However, I also wondered why the early-1900s hymnal came into being. The controversy over style is certainly not a new issue.

This issue of worship styles is one of the most controversial subjects in the church today. If you want to stir up an argument, just bring up this topic at your church's next potluck dinner and see what happens. It won't take long to find yourself in a heated debate.

So why is there such a controversy over worship style? Well, I don't really want to say this (and you don't really want to hear it), but let's face it: we're selfish. "For *everyone* looks out for *his own interests*, not those of Jesus Christ" (Philippians 2:21, author's emphasis). When I was in school "everyone" meant "everyone." There don't seem to be any loopholes in that. It certainly appears to be all-inclusive. By nature we are selfish, and we have a knack for demonstrating that fact.

We want things our way. We have our preferences and likes that we're sure are more correct than anyone else's preferences and likes. The bottom line in getting past this is to recognize that ultimately worship is not for us.

A few years ago I attended a conference where one of the speakers shared a powerful story. He had been in another city on business with a friend. Since they were there over the weekend, they decided to attend church on Sunday morning. They found a nearby church and went to the service. As they left the service that day, the friend turned to the man and said, "You know, I really enjoyed the sermon there this morning, but I didn't get much out of the worship." The man thought for a moment and then looked at his friend and asked, "Have you ever considered what that's got to do with anything?"

What he was saying was, "Who is the worship for?" Worship is not *for* us. Worship—in its truest sense—is directed toward God. It is not for the worshiper. It is for the One being worshiped.

Not long ago I read an article by a Christian man who travels frequently for his job. One weekend, in yet another city, he visited a church. Before the service he introduced himself to the pastor. They talked briefly. During the service, as he often does, the man made mental notes of the things that he enjoyed and the things with which he, as a visitor, felt uncomfortable. After the service he spoke with the pastor again and mentioned that he had a couple of suggestions of things they could do to improve the service. The pastor responded with a question for which the man was totally unprepared:

"What was it about the service that you think *God* didn't like?"

That's the real question for all of us. We must not let our personal biases skew the answer. I may not be completely enamored with the style of worship utilized by the church down the road. However, since the worship isn't for *me*, what difference does it make if *I* don't like the style? If our worship is truly directed toward God, then issues of style are far less important. What makes *me* happy is not necessarily what pleases the Lord.

So why am I saying all of this as a preliminary point to a book about renewing your church's worship? After all, if the worship is not for us, what difference does the style make? There are two important factors to consider. First, this book is being written to those in leadership. You may not be a pastor, but if you are endeavoring to help your church move forward in a style of worship that is more relevant to the culture, then you are helping to lead. You are, in essence, a leader. This means that you should recognize some things that the average person in the congregation may not recognize. By sharing these things with you, I am attempting to broaden your perspective on worship.

Second, most people—Christians as well as non-Christians—are not mature enough simply to be content with whatever style of worship is being used. (Remember, "everyone looks out for his own interests.") In fact, we have been so tainted by our culture's consumerism that it is nearly impossible to leave that mentality—what's in it for me?—behind when we enter a church building.

Because of this, we should try to bring the people along gently, using a setting and style of music that is understandable to them.

Please recognize that I am not saying we should just go along with whatever the majority thinks about every issue in the church. In His Word God has given us clear mandates about many issues. However, in the absence of clear mandates, it makes much more sense to create an atmosphere to which people can relate rather than using an archaic form of worship that has little relevance to our society.

This chapter really comes down to this point: why do you want to make a change? Some of those selfish people in your church are going to be very unhappy with the change. Things could even get ugly in the process. So why would you want to go through all that? What is your motivation for making a change?

In the very first chapter we discussed the idea of making a change simply so the people won't be quite so lethargic. Clearly this is wrong. What are other reasons churches consider changing how they worship? Some do it to "keep up with the competition." Churches in the area are having success with a more contemporary-style worship service, and there is pressure to start a similar service. Perhaps your goal is to reach younger people.

Richard Webb, former associate director of evangelism for the Evangelical Lutheran Church in America (ELCA), has twice been through a worship style transition in his own church. He has also had the opportunity to be involved with numerous other churches who have gone through a similar change. When I asked him to name the most important things a church should know before embarking on a transition, he said, "The first thing I'd tell them is that they need to know the biblical 'why' for the transition. Just because you want to make a change is not good enough. Personal preference is also not good enough. The primary reason we make any changes in worship is to help seeker and believer alike experience the truth and grace of Jesus. If that's the reason you want to make the change, you're on the right track."

There's the real motivation: to help seeker and believer alike experience the truth and grace of Jesus. When that is your motivation, it is much easier to handle the situation when people complain. The difficult times are not quite so difficult. Contentious people seem much less contentious if your desire is to see them experience the truth and grace of Jesus.

With this as a starting point, let's look at how to go about it.

CHAPTER 5

PUTTING AN END TO THE BLESS-ME CLUB

🌿 *Casting the Vision and Setting Goals*

Not long ago I went on a field trip with my daughter's school class. We went to the St. Louis Zoo, reportedly one of the best zoos in the nation and definitely the best free zoo. My job that day was to chaperone four first and second graders. (I gained a tremendous new respect for their teacher.)

We initially did a couple things together with the entire class. After that, however, we were on our own, so I asked the kids what they wanted to see. We ended up with quite a list. After eliminating the sights that two or more were vehemently opposed to ("Ooooh, not the reptile house!!!"), we set out to see the things they had requested. Having been to the St. Louis Zoo many times over the years, I knew the way to each of the places they wanted to go. I led the way to each exhibit, making certain we took the most direct route. They, on the other hand, had no idea how to get to our destinations. Because of this, they crisscrossed paths, climbed over things, ran in circles, and expended a lot of energy.

If we honestly don't know where we're going when we move a church forward in worship, we too will expend an awful lot of wasted energy. (By the way, kids at the zoo expending lots of energy is a good thing. Wasting time and energy in the church because you really don't know where you're going is not.) We need to have some kind of goal, some vision of what we want to see happening. How can we possibly know if we are going in the right direction if we don't have something for which we are aiming? How will we know we are actually making progress unless we have some kind of goal?

I travel and regularly minister in Bible-believing churches of nearly every background all over North America. I have noticed something in my travels that is worth noting here. In churches that have a clearly defined and frequently articulated vision, there is almost always more sense of purpose. The people are more involved and feel as though what they are doing counts for something bigger than their own little lives.

Without vision the church becomes simply a bless-me club. All we think about is *our* church. We want the services to be enjoyable to *us*. No thought is given to reaching the lost and others God might be drawing to our congregation. The whole picture becomes focused on me. Churches like this remind me of a room full of two-year-olds. "No, mine!" "I want it!" "It's mine!"

Please understand that this is not specifically a congregational problem. This is a leadership problem. If we as leaders have not given our flock a vision, how could we expect them to focus outside of themselves? Yes, they are immature, but lack of leadership has helped maintain that immaturity. If the people act like two-year-olds because they have no vision, we leaders need to shoulder the majority of the responsibility.

One pastor made a statement I had never considered before: "Whenever the church is making any kind of transition and things don't go well—people are unsupportive, they refuse to budge from where they've been, they don't seem to grasp where we're headed—it is usually a leadership problem." I realized he is correct. In general, the failures that I have encountered in churches have usually been because leaders had not done a good job of communicating the vision. And when a church has become inwardly focused because it has no vision, it is in a dangerous place.

A clearly articulated, overall vision is essential, and in order to move forward in worship, that overall vision must include a clearly delineated vision for worship ministry. It must include tangible and specific goals, and these should include goals for leaders as well as the congregation.

As you consider your goals, please keep in mind that you should not simply copy what someone else has done. Your church has a unique fingerprint. The people in your church have gone through experiences, individually and collectively, that make you different from any other church. Because of this, it is essential to carefully and prayerfully consider the best path for *your* church.

John Barcanic, a former full-time worship pastor, has assisted or consulted with several churches in the Chicago area regarding worship. He offered these thoughts: "It's important to consider the whole service when talking about worship style. Everything from the music, to how we dress, to which Bible translation will be used, to the way we speak from the platform, to how we encourage the congregation to participate should be discussed." The more specifics you can nail down early, the better off you will be in the long run.

In addition to Barcanic's suggestions, let's look at some other specific ideas you might want to consider. If you are considering starting a more culturally relevant service, what kind of time frame do you have in mind to begin? What things will you do to prepare for starting such a service? For whom is the service geared? You will need to do things differently if you are going after teens and twenty-somethings than if your target is those in their forties and fifties.

Maybe the entire idea of a renewed style of worship is brand new to your church. You might consider goals for beginning a worship music ministry. What instruments will you utilize? How will you recruit people? What level of proficiency will they need to have? Will they rehearse weekly? If so, when and where? How many people do you want involved in the first year? What about in five years?

Perhaps your church has been very formal, and one of your one-year goals is that you want to see at least a few people worshiping in a more demonstrative way (raising hands, kneeling, etc.) than they have in the past. This could be a goal for you. Or perhaps you'll desire something as simple as incorporating two worship choruses into your regular corporate gathering.

These are just a few examples. There are literally thousands of possibilities and variations of goals that might be appropriate for your setting.

One of the important factors in creating goals is getting the people involved. If you ask for their input, then when the final goals are formulated, they feel as though they have had a part in the process. I am not recommending everyone voting on the goals. Nothing in Scripture suggests that a church should be a democracy (although if that is the structure of your church, then you will most likely need to work within that framework). However, asking for people's thoughts and ideas gives them ownership in the process.

Once you have your goals listed, they must be clearly articulated to the congregation. The more clearly articulated your vision, the better chance you have for actually reaching it. Further, it is vital that the vision be put in terms to which people can relate. Rev. Joel Christiansen of the Lutheran Church of Webster Gardens (Missouri Synod) in St. Louis, Missouri, said it like this:

One of the things that effective leaders do is to take the stories from the past and use them to connect with the future. For instance, it is valuable for me to refer to our heritage—perhaps quotes by Martin Luther or even examples from the history of this particular congregation—and to use those to give positive examples to where we are going. For example, when we have considered changing our worship services, I have referred to a word from our Lutheran Confessions that says, "We believe, teach and confess that the community of God in every locality and every age has authority to change such ceremonies according to circumstance, as it may be most profitable and edifying to the community of God." With this historical precedent, changing the service should not be seen as sacrilegious, but as a responsibility of the congregation.

Recently we were discussing the importance of technology and communicating effectively to the people in our day and culture. Someone had discovered an old LP that had been used by our church in the late fifties or early sixties to distribute to the community. Here was an example of our church using some of the latest technological developments of their day to reach out to the community. Being faithful to our past causes us to continue to do the same today. Sharing this helped people understand that our use of technology today has precedent in our congregation.

Offering a positive example from your specific tradition or Christian history in general will help people embrace the vision. This can help the congregation grasp the goals and vision.

Further, you must not come up with goals and then hide them in a file somewhere. Where you are headed as a congregation must be spoken regularly. A one-time mention won't do it. People must hear it and see it over and over and over (and over) before it will really sink in. Things like newsletters, bulletin boards, video projection, and letters to the congregation can help drive home the point.

I like to think of this in terms of learning a new song. When I was responsible for the worship ministry at our church, I generally learned new songs because I heard them and liked them. After hearing a song several times, either on a recording or on the radio, I would begin to sing along with it. If the lyrics were aligned with the direction God was taking our congregation, then I would generally take the time to learn the song on my own. Then I would teach the song to the worship ministry team. Finally, after we had rehearsed it together for at least a few weeks, we introduced it to the congregation.

When we introduce a new song at our church, we don't just use it once and then forget about it for a few weeks. If we do that, the next time we use the song we'll need to introduce it all over again. Instead we generally use a song for three weeks in a row. After that we can set it aside for a while, but when we use it again in a couple of months, the people will have a better chance of remembering it.

By this point, it is no longer a new song to me. From my perspective it is an old song. Between my own personal learning of the song, teaching it to the music ministry team, and then finally using it in a congregational setting, I have sung this song scores—if not hundreds—

of times. It is not new to me. However, the people are just beginning to be excited about it. They are grasping the meaning of its words and singing them with gusto.

The process of imparting vision is much the same. When leaders are to the point where they are tired of saying it, the people are just beginning to catch the vision and make it their own. One experienced pastor said, "You need to communicate the vision until you're almost nauseous from it." Don't stop. Keep going. Speak it again and again and again.

Give the people something with an honest biblical foundation to shoot for. Define God's goals for your church and present them clearly. You may be surprised how motivated people can be when they have a vision.

CHAPTER 6

UNITED WE STAND

🔥 *Leadership Must Stand Together through Worship Transition*

When endeavoring to make a transition in your worship style, it is imperative that those in leadership be on the same page. They all need to be headed in the same direction. When you begin to approach this idea about style and where you're going as a congregation, the congregational leaders absolutely must be in alignment.

Unfortunately, a common situation is that the person in the music leadership position (worship leader, song leader, minister of music, chorister—whatever the title) is the one who has a more traditional bent. Often that person bucks against the changes that are being proposed. One church I encountered told of having a full-time staff person who was responsible for worship. This man had been at the church for more than thirty years and was very influential in the congregation. The dilemma was that he was not only opposed to a more contemporary style of worship but openly rebellious against it.

When this happens, some kind of change needs to occur. Either the person needs to willingly lay aside his or her agenda for the good of the church or he or she needs to step aside for the good of the church. There will be no honest forward movement when a key leader is opposed to the change in direction.

A church's leaders do not necessarily need to be unanimous about each step. There may be honest disagreement about certain steps during the journey. However, they must be unified about where they are headed; they must agree that they are moving toward a more culturally relevant style of worship. When they know and agree about the major, overarching goals and the vision, many of the specifics can be ironed out along the way.

John Chevalier, former worship pastor at Redwood Evangelical Covenant Church in Santa Rosa, California, said, "The church leadership needs to be in agreement as to where you are going…. Maybe not in the everyday operations of the worship department, but certainly in the directional aspects of where you are headed. After all, they (leadership folks) are the ones who will be fielding the complaints as soon as those cards and letters start coming!" He's right. Complaints will come. Because of this, leaders must be united in their direction.

In this context, another important consideration is to be very careful when hiring for a worship leadership position. The person you are considering must embrace the worship philosophy of your church. Don't expect a new worship leader to "grow into it." Don't be swayed by the person's talent and think that he or she will eventually see things your way. The new worship leader absolutely must be in sync with the church's worship philosophy, or there *will* be trouble ahead. I do not believe it would be possible for me to overstress this point.

I can't even recall all the horror stories I have heard about this topic. A church has searched for and found an amazingly gifted worship leader. He has all the necessary musical talent. His people skills are good. He may even have organizational ability (but don't count on it!). The one factor that seems somewhat awry is that his philosophy of worship does not line up with that of the church. Uh-oh. I don't even want to think about how ugly this situation could be a year from his hiring.

In one such case, the very gifted worship leader began to think that his ideas were ultimately far better than those in leadership of the church. In the brief time he had been with the church, his talents and personality had gained him great influence in the congregation. He decided to leave to start a church that "really worships." In the process, he took many of the people with him.

I know of another situation where the relatively new worship leader slowly but surely began to undermine everything the pastor tried to do in the church. Every suggestion was readily acknowledged and then totally ignored. I won't go into the details, but it wasn't pretty.

I wish these stories weren't true. More, I wish they were isolated incidents. They are not. These are but a couple in the scores of similar stories I've heard in my travels.

Let me make this perfectly clear. In the long run, it would be far better to hire a worship leader who wholeheartedly embraces the church's philosophy of worship but whose musical abilities are not quite as good. I recommend that if you are considering hiring someone, highlight these few paragraphs and make anyone who has anything to do with the hiring process read them.

Further, consistent communication among the leadership of the church throughout the course of the transition is imperative. Undoubtedly there will need to be course corrections along the way. There will be bumps and detours as you proceed. These need to be discussed while they are happening.

Several people I interviewed felt that the worship leader can have too much authority in the transition process. One worship leader said he was given lots of freedom—too much freedom—in making the decisions of how fast or slow to go with the transition and what new innovations should come next. In retrospect he realized that if he had had consistent input from the rest of the church leadership, the overall transition would have gone much more smoothly. Instead of making all the decisions on his own, he would have found safety in a "multitude of counselors" (Proverbs 24:6 KJV).

Regular leadership meetings (every other week is the absolute minimum) are crucial. Discussions should include what feedback has been received, how things have gone so far, what steps are next, how those steps will be implemented, etc. Do not leave these things to chance. If you desire to come through this transition with the majority of the congregation and the leadership intact, regular communication is essential.

Finally, in evaluating your progress, there are some things to keep in mind. First, don't give in to the temptation to take major steps backward because of criticism. If you honestly believe that you are heading in the direction you need to be going as a church, then negative feedback is no reason to severely alter your course. Keep in mind that you will almost certainly encounter some criticism. Every church leader I talked with whose church has been through this kind of transition said they had at least some opposition. Many had quite a lot.

When three or four different people approach you after a service and tell you how much they dislike the changes, the natural tendency is to revert to the old way of doing things. It will, after all, keep people from being upset. Don't do it! If your goal is just to keep people happy, you are not being true to your calling. Jesus didn't come to make people happy. In fact, during His visible earthly ministry, He made many people quite upset. If you will bend at the first sign of opposition, don't even bother starting into a transition, because you *will* be opposed at some point. Just stay the course. Keep on going. "If you falter in times of trouble, how small is your strength!" (Proverbs 24:10). As we've discussed already, go slowly and let love be your motivation, but don't give up just because someone disagrees with the direction.

Second, you will encounter technological glitches. There will at some point be feedback from your fancy new sound system. At another time (hopefully not in the same service) one or more of the microphones will not work. During one of your services, the video projection system will act up (this is usually due to operator error, but it will happen). Some morning one of your most crucial instrumentalists won't show up, or just as bad, will play much too loudly. I could continue, but you get the idea.

When these things happen, people will let you know about it. "We never had that awful noise before we started making these changes." "The words are *always* correct in the hymnals. Why don't we just use them instead of that projector."

Although I could reiterate my previous point about not giving up because of criticism, what I really want to convey is that these things are going to happen. You can do everything possible to assure that all goes smoothly, but mistakes will be made. Don't get discouraged when these things happen. Simply handle it as gracefully as you can and go on.

Through tumultuous times, the church leaders need to bolster one another. Keep encouraging each other that you are indeed going to make it. Stick together and the final outcome will be worth the effort.

CHAPTER 7

SHOUTING AND CLAPPING AND DANCING, OH MY!

❦ Teaching a Biblical Perspective of Worship

I am about to make a statement that may shock you. Ready? The overwhelming majority of people don't like change. Profound, huh?

You're probably thinking, *I know that. Everyone knows that.* It would be accurate to say that the average person in our society would agree that most people don't like change. However, we often can't understand why our congregations are unwilling to take the steps we are requesting. After all, these are good things for a better tomorrow. In the long run, these are things that will be helpful in positioning ourselves to achieve our mission. People's reluctance to make changes baffles us.

Many churches miss a key point in trying to move forward in worship transitions. They never include thorough teaching about the biblical concepts of worship. Along with imparting the specific vision for your congregation, it is essential to make sure people understand the reason *why* you are changing. After all, they may reason, what's wrong with the way we've been doing things? People won't find the motivation to change without understanding the "why" behind it.

A common mistake that pastors make in considering teaching about worship is assuming too much knowledge on the part of the folks in their congregations. The most prudent course of action is to assume that the people know absolutely nothing about true, biblical worship. This is not as strange as it may seem. I was honestly surprised at the number of pastors who told me they realized after starting through the transition process that many of their people really didn't even know what Scripture says regarding worship. They had assumed too much knowledge on the part of their congregation members.

One pastor told me that he had recently preached a sermon on worship. A few days later, a man came up to him and said, "Sunday was the first time anyone really taught me *how* to worship." This man had been in church nearly all his life and had even been a part of this church for quite some time. However, he had never really been instructed before about worship.

The reality is that many people in church today take more of the cues about what is acceptable and proper in worship from their experience in church as children instead of from what the Bible says. Keep in mind that all of these experiences may not be wrong. However, they may not all be biblical, either.

Marva Dawn, author of *Reaching Out Without Dumbing Down* and *A Royal "Waste" of Time*, recently made these comments about the importance of education in helping to alleviate the controversy over worship styles:

> We need to put larger components of what worship is in our education classes for new members. We should have Bible classes on the essence of worship. We can make better use of biblical texts on worship when they occur in the lectionary. We can put comments in the bulletin that help educate people about worship. It needs to come from all angles... Educate, educate, educate, educate and educate."[1]

In the same interview, Dawn says that for a long time we have *failed* to educate people about worship. She's right. We have neglected a very important aspect of our duty as the church, and now we are reaping what we have sown. There is often controversy because people are not educated about true, biblical worship. Christian researcher George Barna recently said, "The major challenge is not about how to use music to facilitate worship as much as it is to help people understand worship and have an intense passion to connect with God."[2]

A few years ago, I was ministering in a Christian (Disciples of Christ) Church in a rather conservative area of the Midwest. The pastor of this church had previously pastored a church in a medium-sized city in Puerto Rico. His was the only English-speaking church in the city. Consequently there were English-speaking Christians of practically every background in his church. Because of their diversity of backgrounds, church members had quite a variety of ideas about worship. For the sake of unity, this pastor wanted to get them all on the same page about worship. He began months of personal study of the Word of God. He was trying to go beyond his own background and look honestly at what the Bible has to say about worship. Once he completed this monumental study, he began teaching what he had learned to the congregation.

Sometime later he left that church in Puerto Rico and became the pastor of the Christian Church where I encountered him. He told me that shortly after coming to this church he had begun teaching the same things about worship to the congregation. He told me that it only took two sermons before people started coming to him and asking questions like, "You're not turning this into a charismatic church, are you?" He never once intimated that he had any charismatic leanings.

Too often, however, people in our society have equated certain forms of worship and certain expressions of worship with certain types of churches. If someone raises their hands or expresses an exuberant joy, many people have the idea that person must be Pentecostal. Unfortunately, we have too often failed to recognize that many of those forms and expressions are not charismatic or Pentecostal. They are biblical. We have relied too much on our cultural bias and our traditions instead of looking honestly at what the Bible has to say about worship.

For example, take a look at Psalm 95:1–2: "Come, let us sing for joy to the LORD; let us shout aloud to the Rock of our salvation. Let us come before him with thanksgiving and extol him with music and song."

"Singing for joy? Our congregation loves to sing. Extolling God with music and song? No problem. Coming before Him with thanksgiving? Of course we're thankful to God. But hold on a minute. None of that shouting stuff in *our* church."

"Why not?"

"We don't do that in this church."

"But it's in the Bible."

"Well, yes, but we just don't do that here."

"But it's scriptural."

"Sorry, not here."

Please understand that I am not suggesting that you should shout to God in every service. The Bible does not say that. However, to be completely unwilling ever to "shout aloud to the Rock of our salvation" goes beyond Scripture. We take too many of our cues of what is acceptable from what our traditions have taught us instead of what the Bible says.

I regularly teach worship seminars at churches of different backgrounds across North America. Sometimes during these seminars I mention that for a long time our church had an "expressive worship" team. This was a group of people who would do hand motions and liturgical dance. The expressive worship team physically involved the congregation in the way that the music team would vocally involve the congregation.

When I have shared this concept, there have sometimes been people who were a bit skeptical about the validity of such a "ministry." When that happens, I look at the seminar attenders and say, "The Bible says to 'praise Him in the dance.' I figure, if it's in the Word, it's probably okay." Then I flash them a big ear-to-ear grin. The reaction is always predictable. There is a bit of nervous laughter, and then everyone is at ease with the idea.

Why are they now okay with a concept that moments before caused them to bristle? They understand that God's Word sets a precedent. It is no longer, "We've never done it that way before." It is now, "The Bible— the standard for our lives and ministries—not only allows it but commands it." A major transformation takes place as the recognition of God's Word is given its proper place.

The goal in looking at these things from a biblical perspective is to cause people to become involved. Worship should not be passive but active. People should not be spectators but participants.

One of the main thrusts of the Reformation was to return the worship to the people. Prior to the Reformation, the worship of the Church was slowly but surely transferred from the people to the clergy. The congregation ultimately became an audience. They watched and listened to the "worship" but had very little real involvement in it. Worship became something that was done *for* the people rather than something the people *did*. The entire focus ended up completely reversed from what God intended.

It was during the Reformation that the phrase "priesthood of all believers" (based on 1 Peter 2:5, 9; Revelation 1:6, 5:10, 20:6) was coined. The reformers recognized that worship was not meant to be a spectator sport. From a biblical perspective, worship requires involvement.

When I was in seminary, one of the professors gave us an assignment. We were to do a word study on the word *worship*. We were required to use all available resources to research the literal renderings of the word. We were expected to search out what the various Hebrew and Greek words that we translate "worship" really mean and then report our findings to the class.

When our research was completed and we all shared our findings, I was astounded at the results. We all came to the same determination: worship is predominantly an action. Worship, in general, is not something we can do strictly from our hearts. It requires more.

The most common Hebrew word for worship means "to bow self down." The most common Greek word translated "worship" means "to kiss (the hand) toward" (i.e., as in blowing a kiss). In fact, according to *Young's Analytical Concordance*, one Greek word that is translated "worshiper" literally means "temple sweeper" (Acts 19:35). Worship in the true scriptural sense is not passive.

Yes, I know there is a time when the Bible says that Jacob leaned on his staff and worshiped the Lord (Genesis 47:31; Hebrews 11:21). However, when looking at the whole of Scripture, it becomes obvious that such an uninvolved action is definitely the exception, not the rule. The overwhelming majority of times Scripture talks about things like singing, shouting, clapping, kneeling, dancing, giving, raising hands, speaking forth words of praise, and more.

We need to teach our congregations what the Bible says about worship. I challenge you to set aside what your traditions have taught you and look honestly at the Word of God. From a biblical perspective, what is worship? Why do we worship? How do we worship? These questions must be honestly considered from a scriptural perspective, not merely from a cultural or traditional one. We need to set aside our preconceived ideas and see what God says in His Word. In doing so, some people may realize that kneeling is not Episcopalian or Lutheran, it's biblical. Others might see that the raising of hands is not Pentecostal, it's scriptural.

What the Word of God says about worship should be taught from the pulpit. Additionally, if you are indeed serious about moving forward, small group studies should be encouraged. Recommend books that express biblical ideas of worship for church members to read. In any and every possible way, we should seek to impart this information to the people.

The only way we will truly make forward progress is when the people begin to honestly recognize the biblical basis for physically expressing our worship to God. This will not, however, come about by a one-time mention of such things but will require teaching the congregation through various means. It will take a deliberate plan of impartation of what biblical worship is all about.

An important final note in this chapter is to realize that teaching these principles must be an ongoing process. We dare not make the mistake of thinking that we can simply preach a series on worship and then stop. Most likely there will be new people coming to your church. Beyond this, however, there is a natural human tendency to become complacent. We get comfortable with what we're doing and simply go through the motions, just like the Israelites we read about in the very first chapter of this book. We have a need to be reminded about these things consistently.

A while ago, during a Sunday morning service, my pastor preached about worship. Please recognize that worship is not a new topic for our congregation. He and I have both been teaching about it in our church for over two decades. On this particular Sunday, he didn't really say anything that was all that new or profound, but we needed to hear it again. We needed to be reminded about the fundamentals of worship. We need once again to be prodded to engage our hearts. By the time he finished his sermon, the people were more than ready to worship. It took no real effort on my part as a worship leader. Our hearts were set on worshiping the Lord.

Don't ever think that your job is finished once you've instilled these principles of biblical worship into your people. Don't get the idea that they will now and forever be ready and willing to worship God at any moment. Every one of us needs to hear about these things again and again. It is vital to make this type of teaching a regular and ongoing part of your church's life.

CHAPTER 8

THE LORD—HE IS GOD!

❦ *Teaching a Right Perception of God*

Even after our people understand the biblical perspective on worship, one of the main reasons that they may not fully enter into worship is that they don't understand God. You can talk about how to worship all day long, but as long as people have a mistaken perception about the Lord, they will never really worship Him.

Many Christians see God as the big ogre, waiting to destroy them as soon as they mess up. With that kind of image of the Lord, they will never fully worship Him. Jesus told the story of the prodigal son to show us how the heavenly Father responds when His child returns to Him in repentance. When we humble ourselves and admit our wrong, He runs to us and celebrates our return. A read through the Old Testament prophets shows this has always been God's heart toward His people. Again and again Israel turned away from God and His laws. Again and again He sent prophets to warn Israel of what would come if they continued to disobey, but these men always pleaded for Israel to return to God and know His tender mercy. His heart is to love and restore His own.

God is not waiting to smash us when we sin. He loves us. And that love is the basis for our worship. As long as we have a wrong perception of the Lord, we will never completely worship Him. However, as we begin to grasp that the Lord truly cares for us in a deep and intimate way, there will come a freedom for worship that won't happen any other way.

Some Christians haven't fully recognized that only God's grace, mercy, and love make us acceptable to Him. They feel they can or must earn the Lord's approval. Even mature Christians can fall into the trap of doing things that they believe will cause God to accept them more readily.

This is a simple, basic concept but, unfortunately, one that we often forget. It is all too easy for us to get what some have called "spiritual amnesia" and forget that it is only the love and mercy of God that allows us to do anything. When people begin to grasp how all-encompassing God's grace is, however, they will find a freedom to worship Him that will not be found anywhere else.

Imagine a preschool-age girl bringing a gift to her daddy. She tells him it's a special gift just for him because she loves him so much. She's wrapped it herself. He can tell. The box has as much tape as it does wrapping paper.

It takes a while for him to open it. All the while, his daughter grins at him. She squirms and giggles as he works to get it open. He can tell she's very proud of her gift and very excited to see his reaction to her treasure. As he forces open the last bit of tape and lifts the lid to the small box, his daughter presses closer to him. She can't decide whether she should look at his face or the gift. She squeals with delight and begins to clap her hands and jump up and down as he lifts her precious gift from its box.

Her daddy works hard to keep smiling and seem happy. He's lifted out of the box a rag—a filthy, smelly rag. Yet it's obvious this is indeed a special gift when his daughter says, "Don't you love it, Daddy? I made it just for you! I worked hard. I love you so much, Daddy. I'll go make some more for you." Daddy is left to prepare to respond as she skips off to bring him more of her worthless, even offensive, "treasures."

The prophet Isaiah said, "…all our righteous acts are like filthy rags" (Isaiah 64:6). All of the good things we do in our own strength are like filthy rags to God. Somehow I really don't think that the Lord cares all that much for the "treasures" of all our good deeds.

Unfortunately we often act like the little girl, rushing to God to offer what we think is something really special. The truth is that all those good things we do, in and of themselves, are worthless in God's sight. He does not see them as treasures. From the Lord's perspective, by their own merit, they are filthy rags.

That's the bad news. The good news—the gospel—is that the Lord has redeemed us and because of His finished work on Calvary, we can stand holy and righteous before Him. All our good works—indeed, even our worship—are acceptable only because of Jesus' atoning sacrifice. Peter tells us in 1 Peter 2:5, "You also, like living stones, are being built into a spiritual house to be a holy priesthood, offering spiritual sacrifices *acceptable to God through Jesus Christ*" (author's emphasis). Our spiritual sacrifices—our worship—are only acceptable *through* Jesus Christ. Likewise, the writer of Hebrews says, "*Through Jesus*, therefore, let us continually offer to God a sacrifice of praise—the fruit of lips that confess his name (Hebrews 13:15, author's emphasis). It is only through Christ and His work on the cross that our sacrifices are acceptable.

Too many Christians have the mistaken notion that they need to be really good in order for God to accept them. None of us will ever be good enough. It is only because of what Jesus has done that anything we do is acceptable to the Lord. Further, it is as we recognize God's love, mercy, and grace that we truly desire to worship Him. Because He has already accepted us, even with our numerous flaws, our desire is to honor Him.

In his book *In the Eye of the Storm*, best-selling author Max Lucado talks about worship. His words are right to the point.

> Worship is the awareness that were it not for his touch, you'd still be hobbling and hurting, bitter and broken. Worship is the half-glazed expression on the patched face of a desert pilgrim as he discovers that the oasis is not a mirage.

Worship is the "thank you" that refuses to be silenced…

Worship is a voluntary act of gratitude offered by the saved to the Savior, by the healed to the Healer, and by the delivered to the Deliverer.[1]

Martin Luther described worship as one leper returning. That's a good understanding. One day Jesus encountered ten men who had leprosy. He cleansed them of their disease, and they went on their way. Only one of them returned to thank Him. Jesus expressed surprise that the other nine had not also returned. Our worship is like that of the one who returned, only more so. We are eternally grateful that God's salvation has rescued us, not just from an awful disease in this life but from eternal damnation in hell.

Besides not knowing the heart of God or grasping the grace of God, many Christians imagine God in a much too tame or mundane manner. Yes, they acknowledge that He is God, but they really have no perception of His true greatness, power, majesty, or holiness. Do you recall the encounter between Elijah and the prophets of Baal on Mt. Carmel? Now there was a display of God's power!

In front of the people of Israel, Elijah issued a challenge to the prophets of the false god Baal. "Get two bulls for us. Let them choose one for themselves, and let them cut it into pieces and put it on the wood but not set fire to it. I will prepare the other bull and put it on the wood but not set fire to it. Then you call on the name of your god, and I will call on the name of the LORD. The god who answers by fire—he is God" (1 Kings 18:23–24). The people agreed.

They did everything exactly as Elijah had said. Baal's prophets prepared their sacrifice and called out to their god. From morning until evening they called out, but nothing happened. Finally it was Elijah's turn. As if really to prove the point, he had his helpers pour large jars of water on his sacrifice. He then stepped up and prayed that the Lord would show the people that He was indeed God. And He did. The bull, the wood, the stones, the soil, and even the water were all consumed by the fire.

To me the response of the people really says it all. "When all the people saw this they fell prostrate and cried, 'The LORD—he is God! The LORD—he is God!'" (1 Kings 18:39). No one needed to tell them what to do or how to respond. They had recognized that God was far more powerful than they had previously imagined. Because of this, they worshiped. As the people in our churches begin to realize how powerful and great the Lord is, their natural response will be to worship Him.

Prolific writer and teacher A. W. Tozer said it like this:

> Worship rises or falls in any church altogether depending on the attitude we take toward God, whether we see God big or whether we see Him little. Most of us see God too small; our God is too little. David said, "Magnify the Lord with me," and "magnify" doesn't mean to make God big. You can't make God big. But you can *see* Him big.

Worship, I say, rises or falls with our concept of God…. If there is one terrible disease in the Church of Christ, it is that we do not see God as great as He is. We're too familiar with God….

I've heard all kinds of preachers. I've heard the ignorant boasters; I've heard the dull, dry ones; I've heard the eloquent ones; but the ones that have helped me the most were the ones that were awestruck in the presence of the God about whom they spoke. They might have a sense of humor, they might be jovial; but when they talked about God another tone came into their voice altogether; this was something else, something wonderful. I believe we ought to have again the old Biblical concept of God which makes God awful and makes men lie face down and cry, "Holy, holy, holy, Lord God Almighty."…

"In our astonished reverence we confess Thine uncreated loveliness," said the hymn writer. "In our astonished reverence." The God of the modern evangelical rarely astonishes anybody. He manages to stay pretty much within the constitution. Never breaks our bylaws. He's a very well-behaved God and very denominational and very much one of us, and we ask Him to help us when we're in trouble and look to Him to watch over us when we're asleep. The God of the modern evangelical isn't a God I could have much respect for. But when the Holy Ghost shows us God as He is we admire Him to the point of wonder and delight.[2]

Although Tozer spoke those words in 1961, they are even more true today. We have seemingly lost the sense of awe of God. It needs to be recaptured in order for the Church truly to worship.

To cause this to happen will take intentional teaching about God. Some have referred to this as simply teaching about the attributes of God. I prefer to think of it as pointing people to the object of their worship, Almighty God. We will never, this side of heaven (actually I don't even think we will on the other side, but definitely not this side), fully plumb the depths of what God is like. Yet, as we begin to recognize how awesome God really is, it will cause us to worship Him.

When we take our first steps into heaven and see God in all His glory, we won't need any classes or instruction manuals. Clearly, our only possible response at that point will be to worship. In the same way, as we begin to get a clearer image of the Lord here and now, our response will be to worship Him. Teaching the people everything we can about God—His power, His majesty, His holiness, His greatness—will cause them to worship Him.

CHAPTER 9

SNAKES UNDER THE BED

🔥 *Moving Forward through*
Understanding and Example

Years ago I heard comedian Bill Cosby tell a story from his childhood. Cosby said that when his parents left him home and went out for the evening, his father told him that there were snakes under the bed. As long as Bill stayed in bed, he didn't need to worry about the snakes. However, if he got out of bed, he might get bit. It was an effective way (though certainly not one I would endorse) of keeping the young man in bed. He was afraid of the snakes, and that deterred him from moving.

Most people are unwilling to move forward, not because they know what's ahead but because they are afraid of the unknown. Change looms on the horizon like a monster waiting to devour them or like a snake waiting to bite them. If they truly understood what lay ahead, it most likely would not frighten them. Communicating and informing people can make a big difference in their willingness to make forward progress. Justin Miller, music pastor at First Christian Church in Napa, California, shared this insight.

> ✴ I always try to turn complaints into teaching moments. For example, at a church where I served previously, an older gentleman approached me after a Sunday morning service and complained about the drums being too loud. I apologized and told him of our plans to purchase electronic drums that would make it easier for us to control the volume. He responded by asking, "Why do we need drums, anyway?" I told him that God had blessed us with some gifted drummers, and I desired to be a good steward of the musicians He had brought to the church. The man graciously accepted my response, and we had a great relationship from then on.
>
> Turning complaints into moments for teaching can be a valuable approach. Of course, having the right attitude and a loving spirit are crucial to making this approach work.

I like that way of thinking. It reminds me a lot of 2 Timothy 2:24–25a: "And the Lord's servant must not quarrel; instead, he must be kind to everyone, able to teach, not resentful. Those who oppose him he must gently instruct…." "Must not quarrel." "Kind to everyone." "Gently instruct." We would do well to heed those admonitions.

Here's a significant key in making forward progress: give the people the information they need in a non-threatening situation. In this way they can make a decision based on knowledge, not out of fear of the unknown. Let me illustrate what I mean.

My home church has never been a traditional church. The church actually began in the 1970s, in the midst of the early praise-and-worship movement. Even though we've never made a transition in style from traditional to contemporary, there have still been significant transitions in our history together.

In the early days of our church, we frequently used upbeat, hand-clapping, Jewish/Hebrew-type songs in our corporate worship times. These were very popular and were commonly heard at our church. Then we realized that when we used those songs, there were people who wanted to do more than just clap their hands but were not certain what else they could do. So we made the decision to invite some people who knew something about Jewish dancing to come and teach us. As I said earlier, I figure that if the Bible says it's okay (see Psalm 149:3 and 150:4, among other passages), it's probably okay.

We held a special Saturday evening session and invited anyone from the congregation who was interested. Not everyone from our church attended, but there were a significant number of people who came. For two hours, our guests taught us a new way to express our joy in the Lord through Jewish-style dance.

At the end of that session, there were some who decided that this expression really wasn't something with which they were comfortable. Were we dismayed by this reaction? No, because they were now making a decision based on knowledge, not simply out of fear of the unknown.

However, there were many people who came away from that Saturday evening session very enthusiastic about this new expression. Then, when we used some of those upbeat, hand-clapping, foot-moving, Jewish/Hebrew-type songs during our corporate worship, they knew a new way in which they could express themselves. They too made a decision based on knowledge and experience.

In offering this evening session, we gave our congregation information in a nonthreatening situation to allow them to make a decision based on knowledge rather than fear of the unknown. You too can help motivate people forward in the same manner. Less formal settings can be very helpful in allowing people to be relaxed, and special meetings, retreats, and other such events can be used to help people come into a greater understanding about worship.

Another thing that can be helpful is for leaders to be an example in worship. People have a need to understand what is being asked of them. When they see it modeled, it becomes much more palatable.

For almost thirty-five years Joel Ragains was the minister of music at Graceland Baptist Church in New Albany, Indiana, a suburb of Louisville, Kentucky. Early in his tenure at Graceland, Ragains helped guide the church through a major transition beginning in 1980. Graceland had been a very traditional Southern Baptist Church. It was also large, with weekly attendance over fifteen hundred. Taking a large church through a transition is not an easy proposition, and Ragains realized that not everyone was going to embrace these changes. He decided first to teach the people in his music department new songs and new traditions. They could and did lead the rest of the congregation in the changes to come. Things began to change. More up-to-date songs were introduced, and people were encouraged to be more expressive in their worship.

Reflecting on his experience, Ragains said:

> There were some of the choir members who felt that more expressive worship was not for them. They held to the model of two hymns, a choir special and then the sermon. It was difficult for them to see themselves as worshipers first and singers second. So I kept the choir program intact but used the first thirty minutes of the Thursday evening rehearsals as a teaching time. I started a laboratory for integrating new styles of worship into our church body. Making these gradual changes has had a powerful impact in modeling worship to our congregation.

Do you remember King David in the Old Testament dancing when the Ark of the Covenant was being returned to Israel? "David, wearing a linen ephod, danced before the LORD with all his might, while he and the entire house of Israel brought up the ark of the LORD with shouts and the sound of trumpets" (2 Samuel 6:14–15). The ark represented the presence of God. It was the place where the Lord chose to manifest His presence. In essence, the presence of God was being returned to its rightful place. The ark had been with the Philistines. It was now being brought back to Israel. David was excited, and he demonstrated that excitement by dancing. He didn't care that some thought less of him. He was clearly displaying what was in his heart. As king he was being an example to all who saw him.

David's son Solomon apparently understood this principle. When the temple was finally completed and ready for dedication, Solomon had a large scaffolding built. "Then Solomon stood before the altar of the LORD in front of the whole assembly of Israel and spread out his hands. Now he had made a bronze platform, five cubits long, five cubits wide and three cubits high, and had placed it in the center of the outer court. He stood on the platform and then knelt down before the whole assembly of Israel and spread out his hands toward heaven" (2 Chronicles 6:12–13).

I want you to think about this scenario for a moment. Did Solomon make this raised platform so he could be closer to God in order for God to hear his prayer better? Of course not. When Solomon got up on that platform and knelt down, he was demonstrating to the people that he was submitting himself to the Lord. He was illustrating to them how they should behave. Solomon was being an example.

When my children were very young, I did not expect them to go immediately from taking nourishment from a bottle to sitting at the table and deftly handling silverware. There was a transition period. However, one of the most important things about that transition period was that they got to *see* others who were able to use eating utensils with some degree of skill. They sat at the table during regular mealtimes and observed others doing what they would eventually do. Watching helped them learn to do it on their own.

As leaders we need to willingly demonstrate what it means to be in love with Jesus. We can't expect people to make progress without a clear-cut picture of what we are expecting from them. We should not underestimate the effect our own worship practices will have on our congregation. We can help eliminate fear of "snakes" of the unknown not only by talking to the people we lead about the changes ahead but also by showing them by our own example what we expect.

CHAPTER 10

SLOWLY SLOWLY SLOWLY

❧ *Don't Try to Move Forward Too Quickly*

One of the biggest mistakes that church leaders make is trying to force the congregation to progress too rapidly. As mentioned in previous chapters, most people do not like change. What they dislike even more than just change, however, is change that occurs too quickly. Because of this, it is always advisable to incorporate changes very, very slowly.

Nearly every person I interviewed in preparation for writing this book said the same thing: "Go slowly!" Each of these folks has been through—or was in the midst of—the transition process. They knew what they were talking about. One worship leader said, "I was thinking in terms of weeks and months when in reality it took years."

I asked Richard Webb what he would tell another leader who was about to embark on a worship transition. He replied, "I'd tell them that it will take time and patience." He went on to say that he has witnessed situations where "the whole process never really sank into the DNA of the congregation because sufficient time was not allowed for people to own the change."

Worship consultant John Barcanic said, "Almost all churches I've worked with in making this transition moved too quickly. If I were doing this in my own church, I would take at least three to six months to gain unanimity among the leadership. I would take another six months or more to talk about it from the platform, discussing why God has called us to this, preaching on worship, preparing the people, etc. Finally, depending on the amount of change needed, I would spend another one to three years implementing the change." He's talking about an entire year of foundational work *before* any changes ever occur. That's a serious commitment. One worship pastor told me it took his church nearly ten years to go from being very traditional to much more culturally relevant. That's a long process. There is no doubt about it, though. Effective change is going to take time. Probably lots of time.

Slow change, though, can be difficult for the visionary leader. The visionary leader sees the ultimate goal looming on the distant horizon and says, "That's where I want us to be…tomorrow!" Unfortunately, the difference between what the visionary leader sees and what the people in the pews see is like the difference between looking through a pair of high-powered, state-of-the-art binoculars and looking through a piece of frosted glass. There is no comparison. The average person in the congregation can barely see the first few steps, let alone the final goal.

Have you ever walked in the dark through an area with which you were unfamiliar? If so, how fast did you walk? If you're like most of us, it was probably pretty slow going. How come? Because you didn't want to stumble and fall, right? When you can see only a few steps in front of you, you're naturally extra cautious. That's the perspective of the majority of the people in your church.

It is vital for those of us in leadership to recognize this. Otherwise, we will always be frustrated by people's unwillingness to make progress. They are going as fast as they can under the circumstances. Remember this, though: the brighter you can illuminate the path, the more quickly they will be willing to move. That's why the teaching we discussed earlier is so vital.

Too many leaders are overly willing to push and shove and cajole people in an effort to make them move forward. What usually happens in these situations is that some people are pushed well beyond their comfort level much too rapidly. Because of this, these people feel as though they have been burned. As a result, they become even more steadfast than they were before in their resolve not to move.

So what does going slowly mean in practical terms? First, it means talking about some of the changes that you are considering as "possibilities" long before they happen. This gives people time to mentally prepare for the changes. "We're thinking about..." causes people at least to ponder the possibility before it actually happens. For example, a church that is considering initiating liturgical dance as part of their services may need to lay some foundations. Perhaps an initial simple side remark could be made about dance in worship as we see it in the Bible. This could get people thinking in a direction they've never considered before. A stronger statement could be made a few weeks later, followed even further down the road by the suggestion of inviting an outside group to visit and demonstrate liturgical dance. Months of groundwork should precede the initiation of a dance troupe in your church.

Second, moving slowly means that you should not make changes that are too radical right away. If you are hoping to end up with a very different style than the one with which you started, be warned that introducing that entire stylistic change at once will cause wholesale rebellion. When I asked one minister of music to tell me the biggest mistake he made in the transition process, he responded, "I think it might have been that techno/rap version of 'Sweet Hour of Prayer.'" Yes, he did say it tongue-in-cheek. However, you get the point. Too radical a shift will generally not work.

Third, moving slowly implies that you should not make all your changes at once. For example, if your plan is to begin using guitar, drums, and a projection system in your services, it would probably be best to not initiate all three changes at once. Perhaps introducing the guitar and using it for a few months before any other changes occur will be better received than a wholesale change. Then, after people have become accustomed to the guitar, the projection system might be next. As I've mentioned a few times (are we getting the point?), people don't like change. If you try to make lots of changes all at once, you may well find yourself with a major mutiny on your hands.

One practical approach is to make initial stylistic changes without making musical changes. Several years ago, while serving Redwood Evangelical Covenant Church in Santa Rosa, California, as worship pastor, John Chevalier helped his church through a worship transition. He now helps other churches endeavoring to move forward in worship. Chevalier had some profound insights in this regard.

At our church we had a number of people who loved hymns. So, rather than change to singing all choruses, the first thing we did was to create a flow in worship. Instead of consistently starting and stopping after each song, we did the songs in a flowing, medley style. We did not introduce a praise band right away but continued to use the keyboard player and just two vocalists. In doing this, we gradually reduced the use of the hymnals. Instead of singing all the hymns from the hymnal and the choruses from the overhead, I led the opening hymn from the hymnal and then put any other hymns that we used on transparencies (later moved to video projection). This kept the beloved hymnals in place but now used at about 30 percent of what they were previously. I was then able to flow from chorus to hymns freely, without having to stop and have the people turn to a certain page in the hymnal.

We did this for a couple of months, just focusing on worship and pointing people toward Jesus in the service. Since we weren't making a big alteration in the musical style, people enjoyed the change overall. It was different but not offensive.

In time we eventually stopped using the hymnals altogether. We did not, however, remove them from our worship center for several months. We had chairs and not pews, so the hymnals were really in the way—on the floor, under or between the chairs. Every time we used the worship center for other activities, I *always* had the hymnals put back. This did not make me popular with the janitors who set up and tore down the room, but I had built trust. I simply told them, "I never know when I might use the hymnals in a service." One day I told the janitors, "When you set up this week, leave the hymnals in the closet." They did, and *I never heard one complaint about them being gone.* Not one. I believe this is because we took the time to make changes slowly and build trust.

Finally, going slowly means honestly listening to the people. When you think you have all the answers and no one else knows anything, you'll press forward much faster than when you realize that you still have a lot to learn. Some people in the congregation just might have some words of wisdom that will benefit you in the transition process.

Christ Community Evangelical Free Church in Greeley, Colorado, has seen tremendous growth during their transition time. Ten years ago their services were very traditional. Today they utilize a full praise band, with video projection and mostly modern songs. Their Sunday services now have an attendance of nearly one thousand people. When I asked Alan Denney, worship pastor, what he would do differently if he had it to do all over again, he was very frank. "Quite honestly, I'd listen more…. I'd listen to the people more and remain open-minded when I hear feedback…. I used to think that asking people what they liked or disliked was tantamount to asking children what they wanted to eat (candy, by the way!). I don't think that anymore. I've learned to value opinions when they are not voiced with a mean spirit. That healthy exchange keeps me from thinking that I'm always right."

That's a really good attitude. If you have it, it will keep you from running way ahead of the people. Go slowly through this transition process, with an honest attitude of love and caring. In the long run, you'll be glad you did.

CHAPTER 11

JESUS DIDN'T DIE FOR MUSIC

🌿 *Progress vs. the Process*

Moving slowly through a transition is difficult, especially for the visionary leadership. One concept that may help us slow our pace is to remember that the *process* is as important—really *more* important—than our rate of progress. If we achieve our goal of a renewed worship service but leave behind a path strewn with wounded, angry people, have we really made progress that pleases Christ?

I would venture to say that more important than making rapid progress is <u>making progress *together*</u> in an atmosphere of love and unity. Instead of just a few of us making a run at the summit and leaving the rest behind, we should always try to go forward together, even if it means we go at a slower pace. I know this attitude of unity pleases Christ, who prayed for such oneness among us.

Recently I read the book *The Art of War*, by Sun Tzu. It is the oldest military treatise in the world, translated into English in 1910. Tzu was a Chinese general centuries ago, but many of his words are as applicable today as they were when he first wrote them. In one section Tzu was discussing the importance of the individuals in the army being unified. He said that by keeping them as "a single united body, it is impossible either for the brave to advance alone or for the cowardly to retreat alone."

There is a lesson there for us. If we will endeavor to promote a spirit of unity in the church, then those who want to move more quickly will be willing to wait for the others. Similarly, those who might otherwise lag behind will be more willing to pick up their pace to keep up with those who lead.

This is not to suggest that going slowly and loving people will guarantee 100 percent participation. Even if you do everything exactly right, there may still be some who leave. Don't let that dissuade you from making the effort. Even Jesus had one of his handpicked disciples walk out on Him. Keep going forward, gently and lovingly.

Perhaps one of the most disheartening realities is that the entire transition process has the potential of splitting your church. Don't think your congregation is exempt from this possibility. It has happened over and over again in churches of every size and every background.

Conflict can come from someone in a leadership position or from folks in the congregation. When making a worship transition, it seems as though the possibilities are almost endless. It is amazing how possessive—and even brutal—people can become when changes begin to rock their comfort zones.

In his wonderful book *Love in Action*, Robert Moeller talks about conflicts in churches. He said this:

> Virtually every church consultant I interviewed or studied in preparation for this book agreed on one frequent source of conflict: people who feel they own the church. Often it is those who have been there the longest who feel that way. Conflict erupts when they perceive they are losing control of "their church." It doesn't matter what the issue might be, whether it's a style of music or dropping the Sunday evening service—when one group senses it's losing control to another, conflict begins.[1]

Bethesda Evangelical Church, located in an older section of St. Louis County, Missouri, went through a major transition. Besides adding a more contemporary flavor to one of their services, their transition also included leaving the very liberal denomination of which their church had been a part for years. In the midst of this transition the church lost very few people.

Pastor Jim Barnes of Bethesda attributes at least part of their success to building trust in the people.

> It is very important to reassure the people in the church, especially those who prefer a more traditional style of worship, what you *are* going to do and what you *are not* going to do. Don't lie to the

people or change your mind about a promise part way into the transition. For example, one of the promises I made was that our early service would remain traditional—the same way we have done it for a long time—and it has. For the first year of the transition with our later service many people were skeptical. They weren't convinced that the early service would remain constant. But it did stay the same. Because of that, there was a level of trust built that would not have been built if we had fudged on our promise. As a result, we have been able to introduce a few new elements in the early service because the people trust us.

Barnes apparently understood that people don't like to feel as though they are losing control of "their church." He understood the importance of moving slowly. Most importantly, Barnes honored and respected his faithful congregation members in making his promises and by his keeping those promises. He understood the importance of mutual love and respect.

Barnes continued with these words: "The number one rule in any change in any church is that the people must know that you love them." The old adage is still true: People don't care how much you know, until they know how much you care. Most folks really don't care how much you understand about worship and worship styles—nor do they even care how much you can impart to them—until they know that you love them. When they know you care, then they are interested in what you have to share. <u>Demonstrating love for the people will be</u> <u>a major factor in a successful transition</u>.

People may not like all the changes we take them through. Some may rebel or even lash out in anger. Don't take it personally. Someone who is divisive does not recognize his actions as divisive. That person honestly believes he is doing the right thing. The problem is that the human heart is desperately wicked (Jeremiah 17:9). Let's face it: we're selfish. "For *everyone* looks out for *his own interests*, not those of Jesus Christ" (Philippians 2:21, author's emphasis). "Everyone"?! Probably more often than we'd like to admit that includes you and me, as well as those wonderful people in our churches. However, people acting in a selfish manner does not give us the right to act the same way toward them. "We who are strong ought to *bear with the failings of the weak* and *not to please ourselves*" (Romans 15:1, author's emphasis).

Our attitude in these things is what makes all the difference. Our actions should reflect the words of the apostle Paul as he wrote to the church at Philippi: "Let your gentleness be evident to all." (Philippians 4:5). Paul's words to Timothy are also vital. "Preach the Word; be prepared in season and out of season; correct, rebuke and encourage—*with great patience and careful instruction*" (2 Timothy 4:2, author's emphasis). We must maintain that great patience while offering careful instruction.

Several years ago I was embroiled in a very serious debate over a divisive issue. Something was being taught that had great potential for division. After looking into the issue a bit, I found that the person doing the teaching had not researched any other viewpoints. I confronted him with this information, and a very heated discussion followed. We quickly realized that neither of us was making any headway and parted company. However, I called him later and told him that, although I maintained my questions about the teaching, my attitude had definitely been wrong. I apologized and asked him to forgive me. He readily accepted my apology and extended forgiveness. Then we were on our way to progress.

Often those who struggle with impatience at the slow pace of a worship transition are those involved in the ministry of praise and worship. They may even resent those who object to the changes. Some music folks view music as the ultimate thing. Their attitude is that nothing is more important than music. Of course they may not actually vocalize these words, but the attitude exists nonetheless.

Let me address this ideology from an important but often overlooked perspective. Jesus died on the cross to reconcile people to God. Jesus didn't die for music. He died for people. If He valued the people in my congregation that much, how then should I value them? With this understanding, it is no longer a matter of pushing and cajoling people to move ahead. Now it becomes a matter of loving them. Perhaps it means figuratively (or perhaps even literally) putting your arm around them and saying, "Let's go together. I know the way."

Let love be your motivation. Don't make having a bigger church your motivation. Don't make having a more contemporary church your motivation. Don't make your reputation as an innovator your motivation. Let love be your motivation.

When love is indeed your motivation, you won't try to progress too quickly. At the same time, when people sense that you honestly care about them, they will be more willing to respond in a positive manner. Both groups will come together, then, to progress together.[1] That, I know, the Lord would deem as pleasing progress.

CHAPTER 12

TIME WARPS
AND ABORIGINES

🌿 *What Is the Right Kind*
of Music, Anyway?

My family and I have always enjoyed going on vacations together. We've had the opportunity to see various parts of this great country that we would not ordinarily have seen. We have also gotten to interact with different types of people than we usually encounter near our home in Jefferson County, Missouri. My kids have found it fascinating to see people who still drive horse-drawn buggies down the road. Seeing one parked at a 7-Eleven is quite a sight. It is as though these folks were frozen in time. Observing their homes and their way of life made it feel like we had been caught in a time warp and had gone back 150 years. Their lives are very different from how most people live in our society today.

I have seen people who have had the same reaction when walking into a church for the first time. The setting, the style of music, even the manner of speaking, can all come across as, "Did we just go back in time?" People in our society today simply cannot relate to the customs of many churches.

Some time ago I heard Dr. Kent Hunter make a statement that struck me. He said, "Every church is culturally relevant. Usually they're just relevant to a different culture—a different time or a different place." He's right.

Music is often pointed to as the biggest stumbling block. Very often one of three styles of music is used almost exclusively in many churches. Either it is the big, massive pipe organ or four-part, a capella singing, or (I'm not trying to offend by saying it this way, just trying to make the point) the plunkety-plunk, Bapti-costal piano sound. Please understand that I am not suggesting that there is something inherently wrong in any of these styles of music. However, where do you hear any of these styles in our society outside of church? Almost nowhere.

People who have been raised on a very different style of music come into our churches and hear what to them is a foreign style of music. That would be like you or me going to Australia, finding a group of Aborigine Christians, and worshiping with them in their native style. It would be foreign to us. People in our society have been brought up on a style of music very removed from the average church music. These folks come into our churches, hear a foreign style of music to which they cannot relate, and they don't come back. Hunter was right. We're relevant, but to the wrong time and place.

Some time ago I heard Bill Gaither speaking. He made a statement that had a real impact me. Unfortunately, I did not copy it verbatim, but the gist of what he said is this: "The gospel has always been the same since the beginning, but how it is packaged, the way that it is presented is always changing, depending on the culture and society." After making this statement, Gaither went on to say that he sometimes has difficulty relating to the type of music his son plays in church. However, he admitted that he could not deny the fact that his son is reaching people that he, Bill, will never be able to reach. We must begin to admit that even though we may prefer some styles of music over others, the others are not necessarily wrong. Music is simply a cultural vehicle.

Several years ago I encountered Dr. Judson Cornwall teaching at a worship conference. During one of his messages, he addressed this concept of music and culture. Dr. Cornwall shared that he had on more than one occasion been to tribal regions in Africa to minister. For the music portions of their worship services, they have what he refers to as "steel bands," utilizing any large metal object they can find to beat on to produce rhythmic sound. Dr. Cornwall admitted that he preferred to have two aspirins before worshiping like that, but he could not deny the fact that the people were wholeheartedly giving themselves to God in worship. It was not his preferred style of music, but it was perfectly within the experience and understanding of that culture and socie

This concept does not give us license to use poor ity music. God is deserving of the very best quality offer. We must never compromise on quality.

even the high quality music of J.S. Bach performed by the London Symphony Orchestra would probably not be readily accepted and wholeheartedly embraced by the people of rural Zimbabwe.

Today in our society there are numerous churches that use a style of music very much outside the cultural norm. Often what happens in these churches is that visitors cannot relate to the style of music and therefore go elsewhere (or nowhere). The truth of the Word of God may be there, but the music is too far removed from the experience and understanding of the people.

I am not suggesting that we throw out traditional hymns. Never! They are a vital part of our Christian heritage. I have seen many churches refuse to use hymns, and I am convinced that this is very much to their detriment. However, to stay locked into a style that is one hundred to three hundred years old simply because this is what we grew up with and prefer is just as detrimental.

Again, we must realize that music is a cultural issue. Why do the people in our society generally wear Western styles of clothing? Why do teachers in the church use modern English instead of the vernacular popular in the 1600s? Music, just like language and dress, is a cultural issue.

Several years ago I was given a recording entitled "The Harp of David." The man who had made the recording researched the style of music that would most likely have been used in Israel during the time the psalms were being written. Additionally, he had obtained instruments typical of that period. Some of these were ancient instruments still in existence. Others he was able to recreate from diagrams and descriptions. He took some of the psalms from modern English translations and set them to that style of music, using those instruments. Some of the songs were quite fascinating, but many were *very* different (i.e., strange) from our music today. However, if we were going to suggest that from a historical perspective there is a particular style of music that would be most fitted for worship, wouldn't this be it? Certainly it would have much more credibility, both biblically and historically, than the music of one-hundred- to three-hundred-year-old hymns.

We must break out of being locked into a certain style of music. We must be willing to try new ideas and new ways of doing things. Remember, no particular musical style or certain instrumentation is more appropriate for worshiping God. It is strictly cultural preference.

Some time ago, a friend of mine, Fern Batchelor, a music minister near Philadelphia, sent me the following document that she had written for her church.

The Perfect Worship Service

After listening carefully over the past several years, we believe we have finally determined what those who attend our church really want in music. Following are the items that come up most frequently whenever this topic is discussed:

- More fast songs in the opening praise time and more slow songs in the opening praise time

- More of those wonderful, lovely old hymns and less of those stupid, dead old hymns
- A longer and shorter time of praise at the beginning of the service, and a shorter and longer time at the end
- Songs to flow quickly into each other and long periods of time between songs for reflection
- More repetition of songs so they can be learned and meditated upon while singing, and less repetition of songs because it gets boring singing the same thing over and over
- More of those lovely arrangements with extra instruments and less of those showy arrangements with all those instruments
- To sing the good old songs more often and to stop always singing those same old songs
- Songs to be sung in higher and lower keys
- The band to play in the middle of the platform where they can be seen, back behind the plants where they won't be a distraction, louder, softer, faster, slower, more often, and not at all

Get the picture? We all have our own ideas about what are acceptable styles of music. This has been true in the church for centuries. Did you know that J.S. Bach was once almost dismissed from his position in the church because people thought his harmonies and rhythms were too sensual? Bach!

It is amazing to me to realize that in years past missionaries from the United States would take pipe organs into deepest, darkest Africa and compel the natives to worship in a style that was completely foreign to them. Is our Western style of music somehow more superior? Does our way of doing things somehow have more credibility with God because we have more Christians per capita? Obviously not. The music David and others composed for the psalms would sound extremely foreign to our ears.

The truth is that music is a cultural vehicle and must be seen as such. Martin Luther understood this when he adopted current tunes of his day and wrote good, theologically sound words for them. William Booth understood this when he wrote and performed songs (with his Salvation Army brass band) in the popular style of his day.

Allow me a moment to give you two illustrations that may help make the point. The first story happened just recently.

Phil Mahder is one of the foremost authorities on church technology issues in North America. He offers consultation through Training Resources, Inc., in Hillsboro, Missouri, helping churches understand the dynamics of technologies for worship. He helps churches incorporate video projection, sound systems, digital audio tools, and lighting into their worship. Before recommending any equipment, however, he always begins by having the church leadership define exactly what they are trying to accomplish. This way he is certain he is recommending what will best serve their needs.

Not long ago, Mahder asked the pastor of a church why he thought they needed the equipment about which he was inquiring. The pastor said, "We are starting a contemporary worship service, and we want to have everything necessary to help us make it a success."

Mahder asked, "What do you mean by 'contemporary'?"

"Well," replied the pastor, "we want to do songs like 'Seek Ye First' and 'We Bring the Sacrifice of Praise.'"

Now, in case you don't know, "Seek Ye First" was copyrighted over thirty years ago and "We Bring the Sacrifice" is more than twenty years old. These are not exactly what I would call "contemporary." However, for a church accustomed to singing songs that are anywhere from one hundred to three hundred years old, these are pretty up to date.

The second story was told to me by a friend who was teaching at a Bible college. The event described took place in the early nineties. To make a point in a particular class, this instructor asked his students how many of them came from churches that had "traditional" worship. Many hands went up in the room. Before teaching at this Bible college, my friend had previously traveled extensively, ministering in various churches. He knew the churches from which some of the kids in the class had come. Because of this, he was quite surprised when they told him they had "traditional" worship at their church. He directed a question to one student he knew well. "John, you have traditional worship in *your* church?"

"Yeah," responded the nineteen-year-old.

"Okay," said the prof, "define 'traditional worship' for me."

"You know," said the youth. "We sing songs like 'We Bring the Sacrifice of Praise' and 'He Has Made Me Glad.'"

Both stories refer to the same genre of songs. One person says they are contemporary, and the other refers to them as traditional. It all depends on the perspective.

Clearly there is not a one-size-fits-all answer. It seems obvious, simply from a demographic perspective, that a church in the inner city of Los Angeles should use a very different style of music than a church in rural Montana. Every church will not be satisfied with a single type of music.

What needs to happen is for us to look honestly at our overall goals as a church. What are we trying to accomplish as the people of God in this particular place? Who are we trying to reach? What is the unique mission that the Lord has given to our congregation?

Once we've honestly answered these questions, we must then utilize musical styles that will help us achieve those goals. Keep in mind that this could even involve using quite a variety of styles. If there is a wide range of ages and backgrounds in your church, it probably will necessitate offering a more eclectic array. (On a practical note: To find out how you're doing as you go along, you might consider taking a survey like the one on page 98 of this book.)

Please don't do what the church has been prone to do for generations: "This is the way we have always done

things, now do them, and forever shall do them. Amen."
Instead, look honestly at what you are trying to accomplish as a congregation and whom you are trying to aid in worshiping God. Then use music that will help you accomplish those goals.

CHAPTER 13

STEEL DRUMS AND PIPE ORGANS

Which Instruments Are Acceptable?

Several years ago I met a pastor from Trinidad. During our conversation he began talking about the steel drum, an instrument invented in his native land. The steel drum has long been a popular instrument in their musical style. This man went on to tell me how, many years prior, missionaries had come to their country and insisted that the steel drum was demonic. Many people stayed away from the church simply because of this pronouncement. Fortunately many churches throughout Trinidad (and those in many other countries as well) today use the steel drum in their worship of God.

I am amazed at how forceful people can be in arguing against certain types of musical instruments. It is as though they have some sort of personal vendetta against that particular instrument. Most of the time any biblical—or even rational—arguments are totally absent.

Let me start by making a simple statement. The instruments mentioned in the Bible represent the time and culture of the writing. Those lists are not meant to exclude the instruments we have available today. Some have suggested that since the guitar (or drums!) is not mentioned in the pages of Scripture, these instruments are not meant to be used in worship. So, since the Bible doesn't mention neckties or modern suits, should we exclude those also?

In 1541 Martin Luther wrote these words in the Bible of his friend Wolf Heinz, organist at Halle: "A new miracle deserves a new song, thanksgiving, and preaching.... The stringed instruments of the Psalms are to help in the singing of this new song; and Wolf Heinz and all pious Christian musicians should let their singing and playing to the praise of the Father of all grace sound forth with joy from their organs *and whatever other beloved musical instruments there are recently invented and given by God*, of which neither David nor Solomon, neither Persia, Greece, nor Rome, knew anything. Amen" (author's emphasis).

Luther recognized that there are instruments never beheld by David that can be used to glorify God. We too should realize that even the instruments of our day will undoubtedly be replaced. At some point we may worship with some strange contraption that we cannot even imagine now.

Perhaps the most maligned instrument in the church is drums. Mention drums in most churches, and you won't hear many yawns. Most folks are passionate about this topic. People either love 'em or hate 'em.

Again, many have argued that since the Bible does not talk about drums, they must not be okay. Well, it would be quite difficult for the biblical writers to have mentioned them since the drum set, as we think of it today, is a very modern invention. The Bible does, however, mention rhythm instruments of that day. Tambourines and even cymbals were apparently popular.

Over the years, when I have been asked about the instrument argument, many have suggested that the instruments we use must be biblical. When I have asked them to tell me which instruments are biblical, invariably I will hear something about the organ and the piano. The fact is that the piano is never mentioned in the Bible. Only the King James Version mentions the organ, but modern translations have translated the same word to mean "flute." Though scholars are not certain exactly what the instrument would have looked like, it is most likely some kind of wind instrument.

The pipe organ is indeed the instrument that many point to as being the most appropriate for Christian worship. In light of this, it is interesting to note that the closest thing resembling a modern-day organ was not even invented until the fifteenth century. So, that means that for fourteen hundred years (not to mention the time before Jesus) people must have been denied the privilege of having "appropriate" worship. Somehow I doubt it.

Of course, the silence of Scripture is not the only argument used against certain instruments. One of the other main arguments is that certain types of instruments cannot be used because, oftentimes, the lifestyle of the people who play such instruments is less than ideal. Secular rock music is often associated with drugs and promiscuous sex. Secular rap frequently has themes of violence and sex. Secular country music...well, you get the idea. These styles and their associated instruments have been vilified because of the lifestyles of the artists.

Let's look at this argument honestly. How many preachers have you heard about who fell into sin? Perhaps they were tempted by money. Maybe they were overcome by lust. Whatever it was, it seems safe to assume that throughout the centuries there have been hundreds, perhaps thousands, who have fallen prey to such temptations. Because of this, do we say that we can no longer listen to any preachers? This is exactly the same logic.

Beyond this, I could also tell you about the friend of mine who happens to be a member of a national church organist organization. He says that from his interaction with people at the national meetings, as many as half of the members are openly gay. Trying to connect certain instruments to certain lifestyles is clearly not a valid argument.

Psalm 150 depicts using quite the variety of instruments to honor and glorify God. I get the impression that the ones listed were just a sampling of what was available. We, too, should be willing to use the instruments of our time and culture to glorify the Lord.

CHAPTER 14

DROPKICK ME, JESUS, THROUGH THE GOALPOSTS OF LIFE

🕊 *Looking Seriously at the Words of Songs*

"How is it that in matters concerning the flesh we have so many fine poems and hymns, but in those concerning the Spirit we have such sluggish, cold affairs?" I find it ironic that this quote is not from a twenty-first-century contemporary worship proponent but from the great reformer Martin Luther. His words are still true today.

One of the most divisive issues regarding contemporary-style worship songs is the lyrics. Many people have the impression that all "modern" songs are sorely lacking in depth. I have frequently listened to a particular Christian radio talk-show. The host's views parallel my own quite frequently. Unfortunately, when it comes to the topic of Christian songs, his idea of modern praise and worship songs is, "Dropkick Me, Jesus, through the

Goalposts of Life." The first time I heard him mention this song, I thought he was only kidding. When I heard him say it again a few months later, I realized there must actually be such a song. Although I've never heard the song, I can confidently say that it definitely would not be an accurate representation of modern praise and worship songs.

Before I go any further, let me make an admission. Although this talk-show host's perception is an overstatement, the fact is that many modern praise and worship songs lack the lyrical weightiness that is embodied in many of the old hymn favorites. They are singable, but they often lack theological content.

Why is this so important? Because average church attenders leave the service remembering more of the songs that we sang than they remember about the pastor's message. Oftentimes they'll walk out of the building humming one of the songs that was used in the service, but if asked, they'll struggle to remember the points of the sermon. I am not saying that this is good, but it is reality.

This is not to suggest that there is no value in songs that have simple lyrics. This type of song is wonderful for connecting with God. There is something profound about singing a simple song of adoration to the Lord. The book of Psalms is full of examples of this type of song. However, a strict diet of only this type of song leaves something to be desired.

In the context of songs ("psalms, hymns and spiritual songs"), Colossians 3:16 tells us to teach and admonish one another. There is clearly validity to using music for these purposes. With this understood, it is hard to imagine serious teaching and admonishing through an exclusive diet of song lyrics that are overly simplistic. We need songs that have solid theological content.

On the flip side, we also should be willing to use songs of a simpler nature. You've probably heard the story of theologian Karl Barth, who, after a lifetime of study of the Bible, summed up his understanding of the kingdom of God by saying, "Jesus loves me, this I know." Sometimes we try to be much too profound and miss the simplicity of the gospel.

Many older hymns fail at this point. They start out in a particular direction and then begin to meander, touching nearly every doctrinal issue imaginable. Because of this, some churches use just one or two verses of such hymns because after that they lack specific direction.

The other reality, one on which we have already touched, is that even when the words are good, the melodies, chord structures, and rhythms of many older hymns are often sorely outdated. It bears repeating. The music is foreign to most people in our society.

What we need, then, are songs that have a clear direction, embody orthodox Christian doctrine, and have music that is up-to-date. That's a tall order but not one that is impossible. There are hundreds of songs already available that fit this description. The sad part is that there are many more that do not. Our job as leaders in the church is to carefully select songs that will meet the needs of our congregation. Don't just use a song because it is popular.

There are plenty of popular Christian songs that have little or no scriptural basis.

Here's a practical suggestion. Personally, I don't generally like making decisions by committee. It can be very cumbersome to come to an agreement among many people. However, when it comes to deciding which songs are to be used in a particular church, I recommend a song lyric screening committee. This committee should consist of perhaps three people who are strong on the theological tenets of your church. Both genders should be represented. Their job is not to render a decision on music. Others more versed in music can do that. This committee is to look at the words of the songs and decide if they are doctrinally acceptable for your church. Are the lyrics in line with the theology of your church? Are they too shallow? Are they focused enough?

These are serious concerns. Not considering the theological aspects is like trying to discuss a measurement while having no absolute. Utilizing a committee such as this will save the musical folks from making theological decisions. In the long run, it will probably also save the overall leadership of the church from lots of headaches.

Although I have not made many specific recommendations in the writing of this book, one that I can make without any reservations is Sovereign Grace Music[1] (formerly PDI Music). Their songs epitomize the description I gave earlier: orthodox Christian doctrine, clear direction, and solid, contemporary music. If I could choose just one source for new music for our congregation, it would be Sovereign Grace.

One very good thing about many of the more contemporary songs is that the words frequently are addressed *to* the Lord instead of just being *about* Him. This does not automatically make it better. There are many portions of the psalms that talk about God (third person), as well as many others where God is being talked to (second person). Both are acceptable. Many people, however, when asked which they think is more appropriate, will say that singing *to* God is better than singing *about* Him. True worship, after all, is directed *to* the Lord.

One important consideration in this overall issue about song lyrics is this: you will never make everyone in your entire congregation happy with a specific song or even a particular type of song. We discussed this already regarding musical styles, but it is also true about lyrics.

Bill Rayborn publishes a popular newsletter, *The Church Music Report*. Rayborn has been involved in various aspects of music ministry on a full-time basis for decades. He has had the opportunity to work with churches across the nation. Recently I had the opportunity to work with Rayborn on a book project, and he shared some interesting thoughts along these lines.

I have tried something with choirs across the country, and *the results are always the same.* I have asked choir members to take the music that we are rehearsing and rank it in order of most meaningful down to least meaningful. Not the prettiest or easiest to sing or most popular, but the most meaningful to *them*. No one is to look and see what their neighbor is doing until everyone is through. Even though I have done this many times, all across the country, the results are always the same. Someone's *most* meaningful song is someone else's *least* meaningful.

Clearly, not everyone is going to agree on every song you use. Some people will always be more moved by songs with lots of emotion. Others will prefer songs that say something profound. Still others will want a simple song of adoration.

Understanding all of this, it is important to have at least some variety, even in the lyrical content. Use simple songs but also some more complex songs. Use songs that contain deep theological concepts as well as songs that are simple expressions of love and adoration. All of these are a necessary part of being culturally relevant in our worship.

One final thought before leaving this topic. It is very important to realize that songs with words that are understandable only to Christians will most likely alienate unbelievers who might visit our church. Please recognize that every grouping of people in our society has some words and phrases that are peculiarly their own. This is true of plumbers, firefighters, salespeople, and, yes, Christians. We have certain terms with which most people are unfamiliar.

With this in mind, we will never remove all of those terms from our services, or even our songs. Nor should we try. However, a steady diet of these words and phrases can cause outsiders to wonder what on earth those songs were about.

As we have already discussed, many older hymns contain terminology that may leave many people bewildered, but this is not just an older song phenomenon. Quite a number of newer songs also have words and phrases that often leave people confused. To the average person in our society—Christian or not—what does "These are the days of Elijah" mean? What unsaved person or even immature believer walking into your service will understand terms like "the secret place" or "the river of God"? Yes, of course you could explain the words before you sing the song. However, you would need to do that every time you sing it to make sure that any new people will understand.

This is not to suggest that doctrine is thrown out the window in order to make everything understandable for everyone. Don't "dumb down" your songs. Just try not to unnecessarily alienate people whom God might be drawing to Himself. As much as possible, try to use songs that convey the intended message without being bogged down in Christian-ese lingo.

The goal of all our worship songs is to provide our congregation with a vehicle to glorify God. We sing praise to Him, sing to encourage each other, or even sing to remind ourselves of the truths of Scripture that encourage us in our faith. As leaders we have the job of making sure the songs we sing are accurate and understandable and do indeed help us to glorify the Lord.

CHAPTER 15

MUSEUM OR COFFEE SHOP?

🌿 Considering Architecture, Atmosphere, and Technology

Once you've made the decision that your church wants to—perhaps needs to—move forward in an attempt to be more culturally relevant, you must decide if that change is possible with your current setting. The question is, given your present facilities, *can you* begin a more contemporary style service? Are there physical changes needed to accommodate a different worship style and make new visitors feel welcome?

One of the things that many people fail to understand is this: behavior in any given situation has less to do with upbringing (although this clearly will influence behavior) than it does atmosphere. Consider a person at a fast-food establishment calling across the restaurant, "Hey John, do you want regular or diet?" Contrast that behavior with the manner in which the same person would act at an upscale, formal restaurant. There is a world of difference simply because of atmosphere. An extremely formal setting creates an atmosphere in which people will behave in a more formal manner.

The same is true for churches. A building that has a museum-like atmosphere—where people feel as though they must whisper as soon as they enter—will not be very conducive to a more renewed style of worship. Let's face it. Our society overall is much more casual than in years past. Entering a facility where everything appears so stiff and formal that there is no sense of welcome or friendliness will generally not create an attitude of worship in most people's minds. Atmosphere will make a big difference in people's actions and attitudes.

Not long ago I ministered in a church that had two buildings. The first was their very old sanctuary (probably built in the first half of the twentieth century) that had wooden pews with no pads and bare wooden floors. The other building was a fairly new sanctuary with padded chairs, carpeting on the floor, and less formal surroundings. The older building was being used for their "contemporary" service, which, although they were in a very rapidly growing area, was sparsely attended. Their "traditional" service was held in the newer building. The responsiveness of the people in the traditional service was nearly identical to the folks in the contemporary service. Not that either was extremely responsive, but it seemed clear that those in the contemporary service were stifled by their surroundings.

The architecture of your building (especially the interior, but also the exterior), the decor, and the lighting will all make a difference in the behavior, responsiveness, and even attitude of the people attending. All of these things need to be considered when planning for a more culturally relevant service.

Please recognize that I am not simply pushing for a very casual atmosphere. A couple of years ago, I had the opportunity to preach at a church that had an extremely casual service. When the praise and worship time was completed, I was invited to come forward to minister from the Word. It was at this point that about one-third of the congregation got up to get a cup of coffee (or another beverage) and moved to sit at tables that were positioned around the rows of chairs in the room. These were not just the visitors but longtime congregation members. I was very surprised by this scenario because it seemed to indicate a lack of reverence for the Word of God. Of course, this is a judgmental statement, and I could be completely wrong. However, an attitude this casual can communicate these same impressions to visitors and new believers.

We are not endeavoring to create a we're-sitting-in-our-recliners-in-our-living-room atmosphere. Going too far in the other direction, however, can be just as devastating to the worship service. The goal is finding the place where people are comfortable enough to freely participate while still maintaining a sense of reverence.

In the Old Testament, both the tabernacle and the temple were extremely elaborate, very ornate. Both of these were designed by God. It should be understood that at least part of the elaborateness and ornateness was to cause the people to recognize that their involvement at these structures was not just everyday stuff. These were places where the people of God were to corporately come before Him. An atmosphere was created that would instill awe and reverence.

To simply copy the design of these edifices, however, would violate our culture. Much of the symbolism incorporated into the temple and tabernacle would be foreign in our society. However, there is symbolism that can be effectively utilized today. Many churches have designed and constructed very contemporary banners, murals, and stained-glass windows, and use video projection and other forms of art that carry a message understandable in our culture. We need to incorporate Biblical messages in our settings but convey them in a way that will capture the attention, interest, and focus of twenty-first century people in our society.

Additionally, the people of the Old Testament were not accustomed to such things as soft, cushioned chairs or high-quality climate control systems. We are. Our society is so accustomed to visual images (television, movies, moving billboards, computers, etc.) that we expect these things. Using overhead transparencies for songs is a step up from people having their faces buried in a songbook, but video projection is a much better (and much more versatile) method. State-of-the-art sound systems in theaters and at concerts have made that kind of equipment almost essential. Incorporating such modern expectations is necessary if we truly desire to be relevant to our culture.

Some churches are able to incorporate these types of things into their existing facility. It may not be quite as nice as a brand-new building, but it can be quite adequate. I have encountered many churches that, with a few creative changes, have been able to add some of the more prominent accoutrements for renewing their worship. One practical example is churches that have simply changed the direction toward which the people face. One of the former side walls becomes the front. Now, instead of a long, narrow worship room, they have a room that is short and wide. Less distance from front to back facilitates better interaction during the service, easier viewing of projected images, and (generally) fewer problems with sound and acoustics.

Many churches endeavoring to move toward a more culturally relevant style of worship make the decision either to remodel their existing facility or to build a new building. They recognize that their existing building was not designed with video projection or modern sound reinforcement in mind and therefore will not be conducive to the style of worship toward which they are headed. Remodeling or building a new sanctuary are their only real alternatives. If this becomes the route you take, here are some things to consider.

Phil Mahder, church technology consultant, says, "Keep in mind the old adage that form follows function. In other words, the design of the building should be determined by the way in which you intend to use the building. In order to do this, it is essential that you plan what you want to do in the building. Get input from all those who will be involved in any type of leadership role in the new service—preacher, musician, drama director, sound tech, youth minister, etc. Make sure you understand what their needs are and how those needs will affect the design of the building."

What you don't want is a cookie-cutter approach to the design of the building. You need to determine the things that are important for your specific congregation. Is the communion table placement something that is vital? Do you need a large space for drama and/or liturgical dance? What are the things that are essential to your church?

After the building is nearly completed is not the time to hire a sound system consultant. When all the plans have been finalized, it is a bit too late to consider placement of a video projection system or theatrical lighting. These should all be an integral part of the planning process.

Some time ago the leadership of a church involved in a building program invited Mahder to discuss acoustics, staging, and lighting. The plan was that the new building was to be used, at least partly, for their contemporary service. After looking over the plans, Mahder said, "I'm sorry to be the one to tell you this, but you won't be able to do the things you want to do in this building."

The pastor responded, "We don't have any choice. The steel has been ordered. Everything is in motion. We'll have to work with it. Do what you can to help us."

The architect had made no real provision for sound reinforcement. Acoustically, the room was impractical for a more contemporary style of music. Additionally, nearly any type of speaker placement would have blocked sight for someone. The lighting was practically nonexistent. No one had communicated with the architect the type of things they wanted to do in this building.

Craig Janssen of Acoustic Dimensions, a firm that has designed and built media technology applications for some of the largest churches in the world, said, "The goal is to get the design of the building to fit the worship style of the congregation, not force the worship style to fit the design of the building." The bottom line is that unless you have this understanding, you will end up with something you hate. The building should be a *reflection* of who you are. It should not be the thing that *determines* who you are.

Ultimately all of this comes back to what we discussed earlier about vision. Janssen goes on to say, "Facilities design *must* be driven by activities (music program style, etc.), which *must* be driven by ministry mission and vision. The mission calling and vision is where it starts."

The bottom line is that you have to know your goals and vision in order to communicate these things to the architect. The architect cannot design a building that is conducive to things you want to accomplish in the building unless you tell him what those things are. Knowing and articulating the things that are essentials for your congregation are absolutely imperative when doing any type of remodeling or new construction.

Whether you choose to make minor adjustments, completely renovate, or build a new facility, there are clearly several details related to the look and layout of the your sanctuary that you would be wise to consider and plan out. The heart of worship is the most important aspect of your transition, but you will definitely encourage or discourage worship style with the environment. Be aware of your surroundings and prayerfully make changes in these areas that will help people become comfortable with the new style.

CHAPTER 16

THE STUPID PLASTIC RING

🔥 *To Add a Service or Change an Existing One?*

So, if we're going to transition into a more culturally relevant style of worship, what kind of transition do we make? This is a loaded question that has nearly as many different answers as there are churches. Are you making a partial change or a total change? Will you continue to do the style of worship that your church has been accustomed to in the past and add to that another style, or will you completely change from what you've done in the past to a whole new way of doing things.

Will you go for multiple services, each with its own style of worship? Or will you have a single service with "blended" worship? If you opt for multiple services, how far toward the contemporary realm do you go? If you continue a traditional service, should it be just like you've always done it or do you contemporize it a bit? Choices, choices, choices.

From a biblical perspective, there are clearly no definite right or wrong answers to these questions. There may, however, be right or wrong answers for an individual church, depending on its situation and circumstances. Your particular situation needs to be carefully evaluated to make a proper determination.

Consider the church that has a *very* long history of *very* traditional worship. Its transition in worship might go something like this: Some of the younger members of the congregation are asking for a more culturally relevant style of worship. "What we've been doing is okay, but we are certainly not attracting any new people. And even some of our own younger people have left because they can't relate to the out-of-date style." The folks who have been around longer are satisfied with things they way they are. "It was good enough for granddad and for pa… and for me. It's good enough for you."

In order to keep things under control, the pastor negotiates a compromise: a blended worship service. "We'll have some hymns with the organ, but we'll also use a few choruses with guitar. For the hymns we'll still use the hymnal, but for the choruses we'll utilize an overhead projector." In order to make this compromise work, the pastor has to promise that they won't use drums. Ever.

Right from the beginning, the service is destined for failure. The older population sits quietly during the praise choruses. They want to make certain that nobody gets the idea they actually like this kind of music, especially in church. When it is time for a hymn, though, they sing with gusto. Big smiles grace the faces of those who have sung hymns for several decades. This is *their* part of the service.

The younger crowd, on the other hand, pushes the edges of the praise choruses. They use some of the most upbeat songs they can find. They had, of course, agreed to the no-drums clause, but no one ever specified anything about electric guitars. Or volume. So they really take things to the limit, at least until it is time in the service for a hymn. Then they sit stoically, some even mockingly. They want everyone to understand clearly what they think about those "boring old songs."

As I said earlier, this service is destined for failure right from the beginning. No one ever really completely embraced the idea. No one from either group was truly gung ho on this suggestion. It is a compromise, the consolation prize. It is like going to the county fair hoping to win the giant stuffed bear and ending up with a stupid plastic ring. It is clearly not something that anyone really wanted. Only now the congregation is worse off than before. At least before one group was happy. Now they are all miserable.

Any similarities in this story to a specific church are unintentional. However, this story reflects the overall dilemma in which hundreds of churches have found themselves. They have reached a negotiated truce in what many have called "the worship wars," but that truce has ultimately left everyone on the losing end.

A blended service is just that, a compromise. To arrive at a compromise, both sides must make concessions.

They each give up something they want. More importantly, each agrees to something they really don't want. Right from the start this is a formula for failure. Christian pollster George Barna said it this way: "The churches most likely to have worship-related problems are those that utilize blended music, which is a questionable attempt to please everyone at once... The reliance on blended music seems to actually fuel rather than dampen the fires of discord."[1]

Please recognize that many churches have utilized a blended worship service. However, from my experience, and according to the numerous pastors and worship leaders interviewed for the writing of this book, the most effective use of a blended service has been for a new service, not a replacement for an existing service. Of course there are some exceptions to this, but these would be churches where the caring attitude described in chapter 3, "Defacing the Temple," is prevalent. Because the people honestly love each other and want what is best for the other, they are willing to bend. In this case it is not so much a compromise as it is an honest caring for one another and a true embracing of the various styles.

A common theme that I heard in my interviews with church leaders was that adding a service was better than tampering with an existing one. (It should be noted that, over time, every service will require some "tampering." To never change anything is to become stagnant automatically.) By adding a new service, you are not alienating the folks who are already happy. They are not nearly as threatened by an additional service as they are when changes are made in the service to which they have become accustomed.

Beside adding a service, though, some experienced leaders suggest that strengthening the existing service(s) is also essential. Richard Webb, former associate director of evangelism for the ELCA, insists that it is essential to pour time and energy into "the existing service so that those who are nourished by the traditional worship service(s) still feel affirmed and supported." Otherwise it appears as though all energy and forward momentum are going into this new, upstart service and the faithful people who have been around for years suddenly don't count anymore. Obviously this is not the intent, but an overemphasis on the new service can make it seem that way. Be sure to validate the existing service(s) when beginning a new one.

Many churches adding a new service opt for the term "contemporary" worship service. I have been in "contemporary" services in various types of churches all across North America. Stylistically, the worship styles have ranged from a few older choruses accompanied by acoustic guitar to full bands with keyboard(s), electric guitar(s), bass and drums, and enough volume to create a breeze. For some churches what I would call a blended service would be quite contemporary. For others that style of worship would be passé.

Again, from a scriptural perspective, there are no clear right or wrong answers. What is best for your congregation may not be best for the church on the other side of town—or the other side of the country. Regardless of style, however, the overwhelming majority of those who have been down the road of transition agree that adding a service is better than changing an already existing one.

CHAPTER 17

ENTERTAINMENT ANYONE?

❧ Being Real

Many churches seem to have the idea that what people are looking for when they come to church is entertainment. This is an error. Folks in our society have more choices for entertainment than ever before in the history of the world. The truth is that they have more than enough sources of entertainment. What they want—and need—from church is reality and authenticity.

Let's face the facts. The average church (less than one hundred people) will never be able to do musically or theatrically what the major concert or television show can do. We do not generally have full-time professional musicians, dancers, actors, etc. Even in the relatively few churches that have the luxury of having such a person, that person is not usually the very best of the best. He or she is good but generally not good enough to tour with the big-name music group or be on a popular prime-time television show. Simply said, we are probably not going to wow people with our talent.

Actually that's a good thing. As I already stated, people have plenty of outlets for being amazed. What they are looking for in church is genuineness.

Recently *Discipleship Journal* asked several twenty-something people about their experience in church. One of the responses summarized it well.

> "I wish Christianity would move away from the 'entertainment' mindset it has adopted in an effort to appear more relevant. Most non-Christians I know come to church after they get fed up with the superficiality of our culture; they want something substantial. Walking into a church and finding a show going on can be a turn off." (Katie, 29)[1]

There is clearly a heart cry, not for entertainment but for authenticity. The average church will most likely not have a large pool of musically gifted people. It is possible but not probable. Again, however, that's not bad. As Katie plainly articulated above, entertainment should not be the business of the church. Being culturally relevant is one thing. Trying to entertain is quite another.

My pastor and I have discussed this topic quite extensively. We are convinced that we should not endeavor to impress people with our musical prowess. Over the years our little church has included quite a number of extremely gifted musicians, but they have never been the focus. Instead we focus on God.

When an unbeliever comes into the midst of a group of people who are wholeheartedly worshiping the Lord—whose hearts and countenances are unabashedly honoring their Creator/Redeemer—that person will not leave the service unchanged. Why? Because that individual cannot help recognizing the reality of what occurred. "These people obviously love God" is not an uncommon theme in the responses of non-Christians who have been in a service where there is authentic, culturally relevant worship going on. There is a dimension of reality and genuineness that is conspicuously absent in most of our society, certainly in the entertainment industry. People are hungry for that reality.

All of this, though, does not give us an excuse to slack off in our preparation or not to work at doing our best. I must state as emphatically as possible that, from a scriptural perspective, we are to put forth our very best effort. After all, Proverbs 18:9 tells us, "One who is slack in his work is brother to one who destroys." Those are serious words. We don't want to be associated with one who destroys because we refuse to do the best job we can. Paul told us in the New Testament, "Whatever you do, work at it with all your heart, as working for the Lord, not for men" (Colossians 3:23). Would you give the Lord a halfhearted effort? Without question, we must not put forth a mediocre effort. We absolutely must do our best, striving for excellence in everything we do. These are clear mandates from God's Word.[2]

Even our best, however, is not generally going to cause the world to sit up and take notice of our talent (although doing our best can keep people from focusing on a *poor* performance). On the other hand, a heart that is passionately in love with Jesus will most assuredly get their attention. People hunger for an honest relationship with God.

Our job is to do the best we can from a technical perspective but to focus on worshiping God. Do the best you can, but that "best" is not meant to impress people. It is, as we read in Colossians 3:23, for the Lord. Yes, doing a good job will definitely help people not to be distracted with the technical aspects, but our focus should be on the King of Kings. As we do this, fixing our eyes on Jesus, people will be affected. They will begin to recognize—perhaps only in a small way, or maybe in a very strong way—the reality for which they long.

CHAPTER 18

MOVING THE FREIGHT TRAIN

❧ *Viewing the Corporate Worship
Time as a Journey*

It's time to spend at least a little time talking about specific, practical ideas for those actually leading worship. The next couple of chapters will focus on that.

Recently I visited a smaller church where two people led worship. One did most of the vocals and talking and the other accompanied on an instrument. They had planned several songs. Between each song the instrumentalist stopped playing, the vocalist laughed nervously and then said, "The next song we're going to do is _____." We didn't really need that information because not only were the song titles listed in order in the bulletin, but we all had song sheets in our hands with the lyrics on them.

So why am I telling you about this experience? Because this scenario, although very common, is not overly conducive to worship. You see, our goal in worshiping the Lord is to focus on and honor Him. Consistently bringing the attention to myself, as a worship leader, puts the focus in the wrong place.

Part of my personal philosophy of leading worship[1] is that there needs to be an initial point of focus to start the service. You and I both understand that when we gather corporately, people come in with their thoughts scattered in a thousand different directions. Junior spilled his milk at breakfast—half of it on his younger sister's nightgown. Mom and Dad had a little spat (spelled: argument) on their way to church. Teenage son is wondering if he can sit with *her* instead of the family. The thoughts are running in every imaginable direction. So, to begin the service, there needs to be a point of focus.

Worship Leader magazine recently interviewed popular worship leader and songwriter Chris Tomlin. During the interview, Tomlin said:

> There's always a tension between having enough stage presence to draw people in and having enough humility to get out of the way and let God shine. It's always a tension because I don't think it's an option to stand up there, close your eyes and pretend you're not really there, that there's no [congregation]. That's not a leader.[2]

Personally, I often begin by welcoming the people and sharing a portion of Scripture or some other meaningful quotation or anecdote to get us headed in the right direction. I'll admit that this process is like starting a fully loaded freight train moving down the tracks. It is usually *very* slow. However, as we go along, the train begins to pick up speed. People become more and more focused in the right direction. The farther along we go, I tend to lead songs that are actually speaking *to* God instead of just about Him. As we progress, if there is a break between songs, I am speaking less to the people and more to God. As the worship leader, I am praying and, in essence, letting them listen in. Our focus has shifted from the person leading to the Lord.

I heard one worship leader talk about taking the congregation on a journey in the worship time. This is a good understanding. It's not just a bunch of songs, performed in concert-like fashion. Our leading of worship should facilitate the people actually focusing on God and worshiping Him.

It is helpful to consider what you'll say between songs. Are there Bible verses that would help link two songs together? Are there things from your experience and learning that you might share to lead into the next song? Would a simple, heartfelt prayer be appropriate before starting the next song? Keep your comments, for the most part, brief and simple. Your job is not to preach the sermon or draw attention to yourself, but you can be invaluable in leading the worship journey. Think in terms of leading worship instead of just leading some songs.

Don Chapman, worship leader at Horizon Church in Greenville, South Carolina, writes a weekly e-mail newsletter (worshipideas.com) with practical ideas for worship leaders. Recently, in one of those newsletters, Chapman said this:

> It's so easy to slap your congregation's favorite songs together and call it worship.... [However] with just a little extra thought you can take your worship to the next level by guiding your congregation through a worship experience.
>
> I like to go somewhere during worship. Start here, end up there. Give the congregation a spiritual, musical and emotional journey. Consider these ideas for planning a worship flow.
>
> Find a foundation song for the praise set. Determine if there's a theme you want to explore, a sermon topic, holiday or a song God may have put on your heart. These ideas will reveal a song or two that will become your foundation for the set.
>
> Is this foundation song upbeat or slow? If slow, you might want to put the song in the middle or end of your set and piece other songs together that lead toward it. If fast, pick another song or two that will thematically form an upbeat opening to your set.

Using medleys of songs—two or more songs together without a break between—can be helpful in keeping people focused. People's natural tendency when the music stops is to look around, wondering what's going to happen next. Giving them an uninterrupted time—not stopping and starting songs—helps them to more readily stay focused on the Lord.

Perhaps a word of caution would be in order here. I have seen many worship leaders string together medleys of songs based only on the key and tempo. No thought was given to the underlying theme of the songs. Musically they worked well together. Thematically, however, we asked God to fill us anew with His Holy Spirit, sang about the second coming of Christ, declared our allegiance to Him, asked Him to draw us to Himself, proclaimed what a great God He is, and even affirmed our righteous position in Him. Whew! My mind was exhausted when that medley was finished. If we view the worship time as a journey, that day we took an extremely fast-paced, hectic trip that flew from one place to the next and on to the next much too quickly.

Instead of this, look at the underlying theme of the songs and put them together not just because they fit musically but because they are related thematically as well. For example, I have often used the hymn "Amazing Grace" and then gone immediately into the chorus of Mark Altrogge's "Forever Grateful." Both talk about our thankfulness for God's great mercy. Or I use the chorus "Lord, Be Glorified" combined with "I Surrender All," because both have a theme of surrendering to the Lord.

Of course you can simply look at your current working song list and see some immediate connections. Additionally, though, there are tools that can help in this regard. Chapman suggests, "Integrity's and Word's *Celebration Hymnal* has a topical index with hymns and choruses, as does Word's *Songs for Praise & Worship*." Another very worthwhile book is *The Best of the Best in*

Contemporary Christian Music, a songbook with more than 250 of the most popular modern choruses, indexed topically as well as by Scripture reference and key. Of course these are just a few possibilities. There are more and more helpful resources like these becoming available on a regular basis. Tools like these can be very worthwhile in compiling medleys of songs for your church to use during congregational worship.

When planning for your worship times, keep in mind the idea of a journey. Don't just pick out a few favorite songs and call it worship. Consider the overall flow and direction, and consider where you want to end up in the journey. Consider not just the songs but how those songs work together, what you'll say between songs, etc. It will make the worship times much more cohesive and allow the people a better opportunity to actually focus on the Lord.

CHAPTER 19

WINNIE THE POOH ON TIMES OF CORPORATE WORSHIP

🌿 Finding the Balance between Planning and Spontaneity

After concentrating on being prepared for your worship service in the last chapter, I offer this chapter as a bit of balance. Frequently over the years, people have asked me whether it is necessary to be mostly spontaneous in culturally relevant worship (a common trend) or whether it is okay to plan everything ahead of time. My answer to this question is generally a resounding "yes." Let me explain.

My kids have long been fans of Winnie the Pooh. The books and older videos have been part of our family life for many years. It seemed logical, therefore, that when the *New Adventures of Winnie the Pooh* came out in video format, we would check them out. One in particular, "Party Poohper," caught my attention.

In this story Rabbit is about to give a party. He formulates a carefully planned schedule for all the preparations as well as for the party itself. Each detail is clearly articulated and scheduled to the minute.

"The key," says Rabbit, "to giving a perfect party is an airtight schedule." He then hands Pooh, Piglet, and Tigger each a lengthy to-do list. "Just follow your list of things to do, and the party will be a success."

Tigger responds incredulously, "List? When a tigger gives a party, he just opens the door and hopes for the best. This way is no fun."

"Fun?! Did you say 'fun'?" asks Rabbit. "This is a party. Who said anything about fun?!"

Rabbit's schedule is carefully itemized, so each person knows exactly what to do each minute. All three friends are reprimanded several times for not keeping precisely to the schedule.

Finally, as the guests burst through the door, Tigger drops what he's doing, jumps in the air, and yells, "It's party time!" Rabbit, however, shoos everyone back out because, according to the schedule, it's not yet time for the party to begin. In typical cartoon fashion, the cake that Pooh has been baking explodes. At that point everything else falls apart, too.

Everyone leaves Rabbit's home, and Rabbit continues to prepare for the party on his own. He cleans up the mess, decorates the house, and makes all the rest of the preparations by himself, all precisely according to his schedule. After the final detail is completed, he opens his front door and announces in a proud, excited voice that it is now time for the party. Much to Rabbit's dismay, no one is there. He diligently looks for everyone but is unable to find them.

Since no one else is available, Rabbit makes stuffed, makeshift friends that vaguely resemble Pooh, Tigger, and Piglet. He offers them cake and other treats and pretends to have fun—precisely on schedule—at the carefully planned party.

As I watched this video, it seemed to me that Rabbit missed the whole point. His comment, "Who said anything about fun?" suggests that the goal of even having the party was about to be missed. However, it also occurred to me that if the makers of the Winnie the Pooh videos were to do a sequel to this story, one where Tigger was to give a party, the final outcome would be total chaos. His idea of "opening the door and hoping for the best," with no measure of preparation involved, could easily be a recipe for disaster.

My wife is an organizer by nature. She enjoys schedules and organization. The truth is that this is a good thing. Without organization and preparation, most things we endeavor to accomplish in life would go awry.

When Paul tells us, "…everything should be done in a fitting and orderly way" (1 Corinthians 14:40), it seems apparent that there must be some measure of planning in order to facilitate such orderliness. Jesus would not even feed the five thousand until they were seated in groups of fifty and one hundred (Mark 6:40). Clearly there is nothing inherently wrong with organization and planning.

In preparing for a worship service, it is right for us to plan out the various aspects of the service. We should know where we are headed. The worship team at our church meets for as long as three hours each Saturday evening to pray and plan for our Sunday services. Our pastor joins us to share his sermon outline. We coordinate all aspects of the next day's service, as well as plan for future services. However, there is more to our services than just what we've planned.[1]

Worship—if you understand it at its most foundational level—is relationship with God. And one of the things that builds any relationship are those spontaneous moments that just…happen.

Years ago one of the catchphrases in the Church and in the world was "spending quality time with family." I quickly realized that, although we can certainly provide a framework for quality time, it is almost always the spontaneous moments of life that make for actual quality time. I cannot go to my teenage son and say, "David, let's spend fifteen minutes of quality time together. What do you want to talk about?" What kind of reaction will I get? Most likely a blank look. However, if we just sit and talk or play table tennis together, the conversations we have can be amazing. It is indeed quality time, but it is a result of those spontaneous moments that just happen. Those kind of occurrences cannot be fully planned ahead of time.

Similarly, although I am thoroughly prepared for a given worship service, I do not always know *exactly* how things will go each step of the way. For example, I am not always certain whether we will repeat a particular chorus. I do not always know for sure exactly what I will say between some of the songs. Very often, however, something will happen during the service that will help me understand the direction we need to go with our worship. Perhaps a particular phrase in a hymn will grip my heart while we sing. I might have the instrumentalists continue playing while I share my thoughts and then have us sing that verse again. Or maybe I have just found out about something that happened to someone in our congregation that would be appropriate to share to enhance a particular theme of a song. My planning has provided a framework to allow for these types of moments, but the moments themselves cannot be planned. They are simply the spontaneous things that just happen, that help us to deepen—corporately—our relationship with the Lord.

Allow me a moment to elaborate a bit further. Elementary school teachers generally have the same students the entire day, but they teach them various subjects. For each subject the teacher has at least a generalized lesson plan, with a certain amount of time allotted for that subject. Suppose on a given day the teacher is endeavoring to teach a particular mathematical concept, but it is not working. The kids are just not getting it. Suddenly, one minute before the allotted time for math is completed, something clicks. The students understand what the teacher is saying. *They* are excited because they finally got it. *She* is excited because they finally got it. In light of this, does she just stop now because the time is up? No, she wants to keep going because of the enthusiasm and anticipation. Their response makes all the difference in how she proceeds. This is a special moment, and she wants to take full advantage of it.

Much the same thing can occur in a worship service. Over the years there have been numerous times when I have been leading from my prepared list of songs but suddenly something happened. We went into a song, and it was as though someone just pulled out all the stops. The people were wholeheartedly and enthusiastically worshiping God. They had clearly gone to a different level. At those moments should I just sing through that chorus once and move on? Of course not. Something is happening that is deepening the corporate relationship with the Lord. Stop now? No way.

It should be understood that there is absolutely no way to plan moments like this ahead of time. Even with all of my careful planning, I cannot possibly know with certainty how the people will respond. As much as I would like to have everything planned out beforehand, spontaneous moments occur in all of life, even during corporate worship.

Let me offer a practical example of this type of spontaneity. Our pastor often gives brief children's sermons, usually with some kind of visual aids. On one particular morning near Christmas, he was talking about the garments God gives us—robes of righteousness—and he had handed out silver garland wreaths. The kids could put them around their necks or twist them around an arm as a reminder about their spiritual garments from the Lord. The garlands actually looked quite festive. Somehow a twenty-something woman—one who is *very* expressive in her worship—had gotten one of the garlands. She wore it as a wreath on her head. During one song she came forward, knelt at the front of the church, and laid the garland down in front of her. I immediately thought of the passage in Revelation that says, "They lay their crowns before the throne and say: 'You are worthy, our Lord and God.'" (Revelation 4:10–11). I shared with the congregation what the woman had done, about the verse in Revelation, and about how we will someday have the opportunity to lay all our crowns at His feet. We then sang "Worthy is the Lamb" with an intensity that was beyond the normal Sunday morning singing. I could not have planned that moment. It just happened.

Please recognize that I am not proposing a Tigger-like chaos. However, Rabbit's precision planning can too easily cause us to miss the real point: deepening and strengthening our corporate relationship with God. We need to provide a carefully planned framework while allowing for those spontaneous moments to occur that will deepen our relationship with the Lord.

CHAPTER 20

PEOPLE AND STUFF

🔥 *Arrangements on the Platform*

An important consideration for any church that has previously been accustomed to a more traditional style of worship is how to arrange the people and equipment on the front platform (chancel, stage, etc.). Naturally, it is impossible to cover every situation in every church because of the many variables in congregational size, physical space limitations, etc. However, by carefully considering the following suggestions, you may find some ideas that are applicable to your situation. These will be especially helpful for considering future platform positioning and for those involved in new building plans.

Worship Leader's Proximity to the Congregation

Some churches have a platform that is quite far removed from the congregational seating, either by height or by horizontal distance. Because a good worship leader will often take at least some cues from the response of the people, too much distance can hinder this vital interaction. Sometimes worship leaders prefer to have a large distance between them and the people, but this is usually because they feel that the distance somehow gives them more credibility or authority (i.e., "I am the leader"). However, leaders who are committed to leading people in worship (as opposed to just putting on a show or being "up in front") should seek the proper balance concerning proximity. For extremely large congregations this may be impractical, but in most churches the worship leader can easily be positioned close to the congregation. The closer the placement of the primary worship leader or team to the congregation, the better the interaction.

The Rhythm Band

The rhythm band is usually considered the musical core of a church's worship team. Sometimes it makes up the entire worship team. A rhythm band consists of piano (and/or electronic keyboard), guitar(s), bass, and drums. These are the basic instruments that carry the rhythm and play the melody on which the harmony is built. (Depending on the musical style, an organ may also be considered a part of the rhythm band.) Other instruments (flute, violin, oboe, harp, etc.) are considered solo instruments and are less foundational (musically speaking). Therefore they aren't considered a part of the rhythm band.

It is important that the members of the rhythm band be placed close together. There is a tight rhythmical interaction that takes place during services and rehearsals.

Without these musicians being in close proximity to one another, there can be real problems with tempos, rhythms, chordal progressions, and basic communication.

Many churches have an organ on one side of their platform and a piano on the other side. Some churches even put drum sets on the opposite side of the platform from other percussion instruments (congas, timpani, etc.). Although aesthetically such an arrangement looks very nice, musically it is extremely ineffective. These key foundational instrumentalists should be positioned near each other to allow them the musical interplay they need (i.e., the bass player can match some of the drummer's kick drum patterns, the pianist and the organist can communicate chording changes, etc.).

Instrumentalists other than the rhythm band need to be handled carefully. They can be placed away from the rhythm band (with proper monitors), although it is helpful to have them as close as possible. Individual miking of these instruments is usually not necessary, although occasionally a solo by a certain instrument may be miked. Additionally, separate your instruments according to other proven arrangements, like those of symphonic orchestras or those successfully used in larger churches that utilize many instruments.

Worship Leader's Proximity to the Rhythm Band

Just as the rhythm band members must have interaction with one another, the worship leader must be able to interact with at least certain key musicians. This is, of course, assuming that the worship leader is not one of the rhythm band members. If he or she is, then the necessary interaction is simple. If, however, the worship leader is not a rhythm band instrumentalist, then certain arrangements are vital.

Most significantly, the worship leader needs a clear sight line to both the drummer and the lead accompaniment instrumentalist (usually piano). The worship leader must be able to indicate desired tempo changes to the drummer at any time. In the same way, he or she must be able to communicate key changes or song changes, etc., with the main accompaniment instrumentalist. Without this communication, the person's leadership is greatly hindered. Simple hand signals to indicate tempo changes, modulations, song endings, etc., can be very effective but only if primary players have an unobstructed view of each other.

Vocalists

The primary vocalists usually consist of the worship leader (singing melody), two or three harmony singers, and perhaps an additional melody singer (especially if the worship leader does a lot of embellishment work or "improv"). These primary vocalists should be positioned close to each other in the same way as the rhythm band. This will help them hear one another and avoid clashing harmonies. If monitors are used, this can help immensely, especially if the vocalists can be given a more vocal-oriented monitor mix. If possible, each of these primary vocalists should have their own microphone to help obtain the proper levels in the overall sound (house PA) mix.

If a choir is being utilized, they can be positioned off to the side or toward the back of the platform area, as long as they can hear (preferably through monitors) the instruments and other vocals. Many churches making a transition to praise and worship simply leave their choirs where they have always been positioned. This can be fine. If it's working, don't fix it.

Visual Projection Equipment

Most churches that have transitioned from a more traditional style of worship use computer projection equipment to project song lyrics onto a screen or wall for the congregation to sing. Under ideal circumstances these are very effective, but sometimes there are problems. Placement of the projector can be crucial.

Two major considerations are important:

1. The words should be easily viewed by the entire congregation (sometimes two projectors are needed, one on each side of the room). Your goal should be to enable people to participate fully in all that happens. If the words cannot be easily viewed by everyone, full participation won't happen.
2. The projector(s) should not interfere with the musicians. Some churches have the projector positioned so that it actually shines in the eyes of the musicians. This can be a real a problem if they are trying to read music. Occasionally the musicians' essential sight lines are blocked. Be sure to consider placement carefully.

Furniture Placement

Although this was discussed to some extent in the chapter "Museum or Coffee Shop?," it bears mentioning again. Serious consideration needs to be given to the placement of furniture. Items that will be used frequently, such as a pulpit/lectern, communion table, baptismal font, etc., need a prominent place. However, exactly how prominent that place is will be determined by your priorities, goals, and vision.

For the sake of simplicity, let me make some primary statements.

1. Placement of anything on the platform should always take into consideration the flow of traffic (people moving about) on the platform. For example, does the location of the communion table (for maybe just one Sunday per month) mean it blocks the walkway where the musicians usually go to or from their instruments? Are microphone cords or speaker wires strewn across the platform, making walking precarious? Will the new drum set block the pastor from getting to the pulpit?

2. Placement of anything on the platform should also take the congregation into consideration. In one church I visited, the middle sections of the first few rows could not see the projected words because of the large pulpit. It rendered those pews, though still available for seating, entirely useless.

These are not rocket-scientist considerations, but they are important. Unfortunately, the little things are often overlooked.

In all of these things please keep in mind that Scripture does not give us any absolutes about platform arrangements. These practical suggestions come from years of worship-leading experience and interaction in hundreds of different types of churches, and I hope they will benefit you and your church.

CHAPTER 21

DONOR ORGANS

❧ The Lighter Side of Worship Transition

Sometimes, when you're going through the transition process, you just need to laugh (on some days it may help to keep you from crying). Here are a few tidbits to help you find the lighter side of the process.

In interviewing people for this book, one question I asked consistently was this: "If you had the opportunity to start your church's worship transition over again, what types of things would you do differently?" Here are a few of the more humorous answers.

- I would not refer to hymnals as fuel for the youth camp-out.
- I would put the brass section in front of the hearing-impaired area.

- I would make sure the people typing in the words for the songs knew the difference between an angel and an angle. We sang about math a lot.
- I probably wouldn't use the strobe light the very first Sunday.
- I would most likely reconsider the idea of using the Atlanta Braves "Tomahawk Chop" instead of saying "Amen." The congregation never really got the hang of that.
- I wouldn't hint that a stylistic change is coming by joking about "Donor Organs."
- I would have asked the older members to stop referring to the traditional service as "the real service."
- I would have checked before believing the youth pastor's assertion that "hula" was Hawaiian for "praise the Lord." ("Everybody hula" had an interesting effect.)
- I would have waited longer before serving cappuccino during the services.
- I definitely wouldn't have replaced the hymnal board with a scoreboard.
- I would have allowed the older members to opt out of the "All Skate" during the offering. (I also would have raised the church's liability insurance!)
- I would have thought longer before agreeing to introduce the limbo as liturgical dance.
- I think I would wait longer before introducing the sea lion to the baptistery.
- I would have let the pastor know that polyester bell-bottoms weren't "contemporary" anymore.

Okay, so most of these did not actually happen. They were said with tongue firmly planted in cheek. However, they might help you and others to laugh at some of the things you actually do encounter.

Additionally, you might find the following to be helpful in sharing with your congregation during a transition. It is lighthearted (actually, it's downright hilarious!) and offers both sides of the story. It was e-mailed to me a couple of years ago, and although it is posted on numerous web sites, I have been unable to ascertain the origin. If and when I am able to find the original source, I will gladly give appropriate credit. In the meantime, I hope you enjoy it.

An old farmer went to the city one weekend and attended the big city church. He came home, and his wife asked him how it was.

"Well," said the farmer, "it was good. They did something different, however. They sang praise choruses instead of hymns."

"Praise choruses?" said his wife. "What are those?"

"Oh, they're okay. They're sort of like hymns, only different," said the farmer.

"Well, what's the difference?" asked his wife.

The farmer said, "Well, it's like this. If I were to say to you: 'Martha, the cows are in the corn,' well, that would be a hymn. If, on the other hand, I were to say to you:

Martha, Martha, Martha, oh, Martha, MARTHA,
    MARTHA,
the cows, the big cows, the brown cows, the black
    cows,
the white cows, the black and white cows,
the COWS, COWS, COWS are in the corn,
are in the corn, are in the corn, are in the corn,
the CORN, CORN, CORN.

"If I did that, then repeated the whole thing two or three times, well, that would be a praise chorus."

And now for the other side of the story.

A young, new Christian visited relatives one weekend and attended their small-town church. He came home, and his wife asked him how it was.

"Well," said the young man, "it was good. They did something different, however. They sang hymns instead of regular songs."

"Hymns?" said his wife. "What are those?"

"Oh, they're okay. They're sort of like regular songs, only different," said the young man.

"Well, what's the difference?" asked his wife.

The young man said, "Well, it's like this. If I were to say to you, 'Martha, the cows are in the corn,' well, that would be a regular song. If, on the other hand, I were to say to you:

O Martha, dear Martha, hear thou my cry;
Inclinest thine ear to the words of my mouth;
Turn thou thy whole wondrous ear by and by
To the righteous, inimitable, glorious truth.

For the way of the animals who can explain;
There in their heads is no shadow of sense.
Hearkenest they in God's sun or His rain,
Unless from the mild, tempting corn they are
    fenced.

Yea, those cows in glad bovine, rebellious delight,
Have broke free their shackles, their warm pens
    eschewed.
Then goaded by minions of darkness and night,
They all my mild Chilliwack sweet corn have
    chewed.

So look to that bright shining day by and by,
Where all foul corruptions of earth are reborn,
Where no vicious animal makes my soul cry
And I no longer see those foul cows in the corn.

    "Then, if I were to do only verses one, three,
and four and do a key change on the last verse,
well, that would be a hymn."

CONCLUSION

So where does all this leave us? We've covered a multitude of perspectives about being more culturally relevant in our worship. If you thought moving your congregation through a transition in worship styles was going to be a simple task, I hope you've decided otherwise. This is not an easy hike. In fact, it is a long journey.

The principles shared in this book should help. However, don't consider this information as the end-all answer. These are simply guidelines from those who have walked this path before you. You will need to consider all the specifics for your situation before deciding exactly how you will proceed on your journey.

In the introduction, I mentioned that this book was awkward for me to write because so many of the issues are not clearly defined in Scripture. In fact, relatively few of the main principles in this publication are emphatic. Most are observations based on experience. Keep this in mind as you move forward.

The two clear contradictions to what I just said are the first two chapters. That's why they were shared first.

Relationship with God is the cornerstone that allows you to continue building. Prayer is the foundation on which the rest will be built. Skip either of these steps and you may as well stop now. These are the undergirding principles from which all the other steps must flow. Don't miss them, either personally or as a congregation.

My prayer is that God will guide and direct you as you journey forward in His grace and mercy.

APPENDIX A

🔥 A Praise and Worship Survey for the Congregational Members

A survey like the one that follows can help you find out what your people really think about your congregation's worship times. This can be helpful for you as you're transitioning. Of course, it should be understood that those answering will most likely be the ones who have strong opinions one way or the other.

One practical point: You can ask people to put their name on their response so that you will know who did not respond. The drawback to this approach is that most likely the answers you receive from many people will not be quite as candid as they would be if the survey were done anonymously.

Part A is designed as a personal analysis of the Sunday morning worship time. It should be understood that there are no absolutes on these things and your answers, although they may be strongly held opinions, are only opinions.

Part A

1. *Do you think we:*
   a. *do too many slow songs.*
   b. *do too many fast songs.*
   c. *have an acceptable balance of slow and fast songs.*

2. *Do you think we:*
   a. *learn too many new songs.*
   b. *do not learn enough new songs.*
   c. *learn just enough new songs.*

3. *Do you think the music of the songs we use is overall:*
   a. *too simple to be challenging.*
   b. *too difficult to sing.*
   c. *a good balance.*

4. *Do you think the lyrics of the songs we use overall are:*
   a. *too simple to be challenging.*
   b. *too difficult to sing.*
   c. *a good balance.*

5. *Do you think the style of music being used is:*
   a. *too contemporary.*
   b. *too traditional.*
   c. *about right.*

6. *How do feel about the amount of time spent in worship on Sunday morning?*
   a. *too long.*
   b. *too short.*
   c. *about right.*

7. *How do you feel about the overall Sunday morning worship experience:*
   a. *boring.*
   b. *satisfying.*
   c. _____.

Part B is designed to add insights to the answers given in Part A. These questions, although they may be uncomfortable, should be answered as candidly as possible.

Part B

1. *When you arrive on Sunday morning, are you fully prepared to worship the Lord:*
   a. *all of the time.*
   b. *some of the time.*
   c. *very seldom.*

2. *Do you:*
   a. *eagerly enter into worship.*
   b. *prefer to sit and watch others worship.*
   c. *ignore worship and think about other matters.*

3. *Do you worship the Lord on your own during the week:*
   a. *often.*
   b. *occasionally.*
   c. *seldom.*

4. *Do you harbor negative attitudes toward your brothers and sisters in the Lord during the service?*
   a. *often.*
   b. *occasionally.*
   c. *seldom.*

5. *Do you feel that you could do a better job of leading worship on a consistent basis?*
   a. *yes.*
   b. *no.*

APPENDIX B

❦ Arguments against Today's Praise and Worship Music Compared with Scripture

"The songs are too repetitive."

Psalm 136 repeats "His love endures forever" twenty-six times. Additionally, heaven's worship seems to be somewhat repetitive. Revelation 4:8 says, "Day and night they [the four living creatures] *never stop saying*: 'Holy, holy, holy is the Lord God Almighty, who was, and is, and is to come'" (author's emphasis).

"The music is too loud."

The worship of heaven frequently seems to be loud. "Then I heard what sounded like a great multitude, like *the roar of rushing waters and like loud peals of thunder, shouting*: 'Hallelujah! For our Lord God Almighty reigns.'" (Revelation 19:6, author's emphasis). John's likening this expression of worship to loud peals of thunder clearly means it was quite loud. Being loud can be an honest expression of heartfelt emotion. "One of them, when he saw he was healed, came back, praising God *in a loud voice*" (Luke 17:15, author's emphasis).

"The songs are too focused on us. There are too many personal pronouns."

In Psalm 18:1–3, David wrote a wonderful song of praise that is contained in the canon of Scripture. "*I* love you, O LORD, *my* strength. The LORD is *my* rock, *my* fortress and *my* deliverer; *my* God is *my* rock, in whom *I* take refuge. He is *my* shield and the horn of *my* salvation, *my* stronghold. *I* call to the LORD, who is worthy of praise, and *I* am saved from *my* enemies" (author's emphasis). One-fourth of the words in these three verses (fourteen out of fifty-six) are personal pronouns.

"We sing too long."

Try reading aloud through Psalm 119, maintaining a steady, understandable pace. Reading the entire psalm will probably take longer than the average church allows for praise and worship today. And that's just one God-inspired song! Beyond this, Scripture also says, "From the rising of the sun unto the going down of the same the LORD's name is to be praised." (Psalm 113:3, KJV). In Israel, where these words were originally written, it's a very long time from when the sun comes up until it sets.

NOTES

Chapter 1

1. Quoted by Jerry Bridges in *I Exalt You, O God* (Colorado Springs, Colorado: WaterBrook Press, 2001).
2. Ronald B. Allen and Gordon L. Borror, *Worship: Rediscovering the Missing Jewel* (Portland, Oregon: Multnomah, 1982).
3. Tricia McCary Rhodes, "Created for Delight," *Discipleship Journal*, November/December 2002.
4. Ronald B. Allen and Gordon L. Borror, *Worship: Rediscovering the Missing Jewel* (Portland, Oregon: Multnomah, 1982).
5. Patrick Morley, *Seven Seasons of the Man in the Mirror* (Grand Rapids, Michigan: Zondervan, 1995).

Chapter 2

1. Donald S. Whitney, *Spiritual Disciplines of the Christian Life* (Colorado Springs, Colorado: Navpress Publishing Group, 1991).
2. Jerry Bridges, *The Joy of Fearing God* (Colorado Springs, Colorado: WaterBrook Press, 1997).
3. Quoted by Robert Moeller in *Love in Action* (Sisters, Oregon: Multnomah Books, 1994).

Chapter 7

1. "How Much Does Style Matter?" *Worship Leader* magazine, May 2002.
2. George Barna, "Focus On 'Worship Wars' Hides The Real Issue Regarding Connection to God," November 19, 2002, Barna web site.

Chapter 8

1. Max Lucado, *In the Eye of the Storm* (Nashville, Tennessee: Word, 1991).
2. A.W. Tozer, *Worship: The Missing Jewel of the Evangelical Church* (Camp Hill, Pennsylvania: Christian Publications, 1996).

Chapter 11

1. Robert Moeller, *Love in Action* (Sisters, Oregon: Multnomah Books, 1994).

Chapter 14

1. Sovereign Grace Music, 7505 Muncaster Mill Road, Gaithersburg, MD 20877; SovereignGraceMinistries.org.

Chapter 16

1. George Barna, "Focus On 'Worship Wars' Hides The Real Issue Regarding Connection to God," November 19, 2002, Barna web site.

Chapter 17

1. *Discipleship Journal*, May/June 2002.
2. Of course, all of this also assumes that a dimension of spiritual maturity is evident among those involved in leading the service. It is generally not a good idea to have a spiritually immature person in that position (even if they are

"only" a musician) because of the influence that person, simply because of the position, will have on others.

Chapter 18

1. It should be noted that one of my personal frustrations over the years is that the Bible is very silent when it comes to specifics about leading worship. There are many fundamental truths that we can apply to leading worship; however, there are few specifics offered in the pages of Scripture. Therefore, much of my personal philosophy on leading worship consists of what I have learned from my own experience as well as the experiences of others. Please keep this in mind as you consider this section. Some of these ideas may work well for you. Others may not. Use what you find to be valuable and discard the rest.

2. "An Interview with Chris Tomlin," *Worship Leader* magazine, January/February, 2003.

Chapter 19

1. For a more thorough treatment of all that goes into the preparation process, see my book *Developing an Effective Worship Ministry* (Lynnwood, Washington: Emerald Books, 1993).

CHECK OUT THESE OTHER BOOKS BY TOM KRAEUTER

Living Beyond the Ordinary $9.99   Eternal life starts now. Are you 100% satisfied with your Christian life? If not, then maybe it's time to start living beyond the ordinary! Practical steps to an extraordinary relationship with God.

If Standing Together Is So Great, Why Do We Keep Falling Apart? $8.99 The church in America is missing much of the power of God because of a lack of unity. You'll learn why unity is so vital as well as specific steps toward making it reality.

Oh, Grow Up! $9.99   The everyday miracle of becoming more like Jesus involves a partnership between us and the Lord. Do you know your role? Do you know God's? Learn the real, biblical answers.

Worship Is...What?! $9.99   In his usual story-filled way, Tom makes the scriptures come alive for today. If you want to understand what worship is all about—or if you think you already do—you should read this book.

Keys to Becoming an Effective Worship Leader $9.99 An in-depth look at what it really means to be a worship leader. These insights have proven helpful to tens of thousands of worship leaders worldwide.

Developing an Effective Worship Ministry $9.99   The A-Z book on developing the ministry of praise and worship in the local church.

The Worship Leader's Handbook $9.99 A question and answer format makes this a great reference book you'll use over and over.

These are some of the most practical books available for worship leaders. They will inspire you and give you a solid foundation for the ministry of praise and worship.

Things They Didn't Teach Me in Worship Leading School $9.99 50 prominent worship leaders from around the world share stories and insights.

Times of Refreshing $14.99 A devotional book for worship ministries. 100 biblical, practical, life-related devotions to strengthen your church's worship ministry.